WHO AM I?
A Book of World Religions

Anne Ler
26 Barcncroft Rd
Liverpool L25 6EH

WHO AM I?
A Book of World Religions

MARTIN BALLARD

HUTCHINSON EDUCATIONAL

HUTCHINSON EDUCATIONAL LTD
3 Fitzroy Square, London W1

London Melbourne Sydney
Auckland Wellington Johannesburg Cape Town
and agencies throughout the world

First published 1971

*This book has been set in IBM Baskerville type, by DP Press Ltd Sevenoaks,
printed in Great Britain on smooth wove paper by Anchor Press,
and bound by Wm. Brendon, both of Tiptree, Essex*

ISBN 0 09 109160 8 (cased)
     0 09 109161 6 (paper)

Contents

Acknowledgements

For permission to reprint copyright material the author is indebted to the following:

Oxford and Cambridge University Presses for extracts from the *New English Bible*, Second Edition c 1970; George Allen and Unwin for extracts from *Journey Into Burmese Silence* by Marie Beuzeville Byles; Penguin Books Ltd. for extracts from *Buddhist Scriptures* translated by Edward Conze and Dent and Sons Ltd., for extracts from *Hindu Scriptures* translated by R.G. Zaehner for the Everyman's Library.

For permission to reproduce illustrations grateful acknowledgement is also made to the following:

SATOUR, Egyptian State Tourist Administration, French Government Tourist Office, Australia House, School of Oriental and African Studies, Government of India Tourist Office, Barnaby's Picture Library, Information Service of India, Victoria and Albert Museum, Israel Government Tourist Office, Juliette Radam, Italian State Tourist Office, Cyprus High Commission, Guildhall Museum, Morroccan National Tourist Office, U.A.R. Tourist and Information Centre and Greek Orthodox Metropolis of Thyatira and Great Britain.

1
Who Am I?
THE BIRTH OF RELIGION

A story—which may or may not be true—is told about the 19th Century writer and politician Thomas Babington Macaulay. When he was only four years old he turned on his nurse and asked, "Nurse! Have you ever pondered the problem of your individuality?" We are tempted to comment that he must have been a singularly horrid little boy. But if we stop and think what his long words mean, we can see that he was only putting the same question that every normal child asks long before he or she ever goes to school. "Nurse!" he might have said. "Have you stopped to ask what makes you into a person, different from any other person?"

When we were tiny children we asked our questions in simpler form. We wanted to know about birth and death so that we could feel around the boundaries of our existence. "Where did I come from, Mummy?" "Where has Grandad gone?" Many parents have learnt how to avoid giving straight answers to such enquiries. "A stork brought you." "Grandad's gone on a long, long journey." When children realize that they are being fobbed off with lies, they stop asking such important questions out loud, but they go on fretting about them. During the period of adolescence, young people are particularly busy trying to find a solution to the 'problem of their individuality'. The quest goes on, perhaps in a less intense form, throughout adult life.

Man is a creature which has evolved over millions of years out of lower forms of life. He is unique in the animal kingdom in being able, as it were, to detach his mind from his body and ask the question, "Who am I?" An animal lives in the immediate present. Our pet dog may be hungry, but he does not fret over where the next meal is coming from; he may be sick, but he does not worry about the fact that one day he will die. It is true that, when an elephant is old and weak, knowing by some instinct that its end is near, it leaves the herd and wanders off to a special place which members of the herd have chosen as a place to die. Other animals may have similar instincts about their own deaths, but there is no reason to think that the most highly developed mammals, like an elephant, could ever form the question posed by a little human child, "Who am I?" The animals are a part of the living world of nature; they do not stand back from their fellow creatures to ask questions about themselves.

Our early ancestors lived and thought like all the other animals. Over tens of thousands of years the light of awareness became kindled. At some time in prehistory they began to ask the question so pompously expressed by Macaulay. At that point we could say that the species *homo sapiens*—thinking man—had emerged. We can get indications of the process from the remains that those distant ancestors have left behind them. First, they thought that it was not right to leave their dead lying in the open air to be pecked and stripped by the vultures and the carrion crows, so they buried their bodies in the ground. They built mounds of stones and earth over dead chieftains so that their great man would not be forgotten. They even left valuable objects beside them in the tomb in case they should need them 'in the place where they had gone'.

As long ago as the Old Stone Age man had become aware of his own existence. He could say, 'I was born', 'I will die'. His brain had grown to a size which enabled him to start the long process of bringing the lower members of the animal kingdom under his control; a process which is just about complete today. But the same brain which brought him so many advantages also brought him anxiety and fear on a scale unknown to any other creature.

As soon as our ancestors were able to look at the world in which they had to live out their lives in a detached way, they began to realize how little they understood about its

Prehistoric cave-paintings in the Hall of Bisons, Ariège

workings. They depended on the hunt for their livelihood yet the supply of game was uncertain. Men therefore began to perform acts, which we would call *magic*, to bring the animals which they hunted under their control. The aborigines of Australia and some hunting tribes of Africa have preserved ancient dances in which men act the parts of the wild animals which are to be slaughtered in the next day's hunt. We cannot say for certain that such dances were performed in prehistoric times, but we can study pictures of animals, preserved deep inside the caves of France. Today artists recognize that these possess the qualities of great art. But the men who painted them were not interested in creating things of beauty. They drew the animals which they wanted to kill; they drew them to bring them within the power of man. Only man of all the animals made magic and art, because only he worried about the fact that some time in the future the supply of game could dry up and that his children would then go hungry to bed.

Whenever man gained this ability to ask the fundamental question, "Who am I?" he began to feel very small and very unprotected in a large and hostile world. His life was at the mercy of immensely powerful forces, which he could not control. In the hotter parts of the globe the sun was a terrifying power. It did good, giving warmth and light, but it also burnt a man's body and dried up the earth. No creature could live without water, but great floods could come without warning and wash away everything. Men were subject to disease which brought suffering and death. Today, when we have drugs to ease most kinds of pain, it is hard to realize that it is barely one hundred years since scientists began to understand the nature of disease. Before the 19th Century sickness was 'an affliction' imposed on man's body by some unknown and unseen power outside himself.

Since he did not understand the nature of the terrors with which he was surrounded, man could only cope with them by means of magic and ritual acts. He danced to make the rain fall, as he danced to bring success to the hunt. The powers of nature, which brought good or evil into his life became spirits or gods which had to be bought off or coaxed into a friendly frame of mind. In the dry, semi-desert places, where nature was sparse, men often concentrated their worship on the sun, and relegated other gods to lesser roles. In thick forest areas, and in fertile river valleys, where nature pressed in on man on every side, men tended to worship a multitude of gods. There were spirits in the trees and in the rivers, on the hills and in the caves.

They were not *moral* gods, which punished evil men and rewarded good. These spirits of the unknown brought good or bad fortune at random—almost as it amused them. Such was man's helplessness that he could do nothing but make offerings in the hope of winning the god's favour, or at least turning away the worst of his malice.

When a man makes an offering to a god, we call the action a *sacrifice*. It may be a gift of food, left so that the gods can come and feed off it. Very often the sacrifice involves the pouring out of blood. If, for instance, a human being is taken sick his family may offer the life of

Australian Aborigines taking part in a hunting dance at a Warrangan corroboree. They are decorated with birds' down stuck on with blood drawn from gashes in the arm. The wooden crosspiece on the head of the central figure represents buffalo horns

Australia House, London

Paintings on the walls of an ancient Egyptian tomb

an animal, in the hope that the god who controls his destiny will accept the creature's life and let the sick man recover. When a whole community feels threatened, it may offer one of its own number as a human sacrifice on behalf of the rest.

Sacrifices, originally performed in a time of special crisis, gradually became part of the regular custom of the tribe. Ritual acts are performed at regular seasons of the year. When tribes settled down in one place to grow their food by agriculture they began to associate their religious actions with the seasons of planting and harvesting. Sacrifice is offered at the time when the seed goes into the ground, to encourage the spirits that control the sun and the rain to give the grain the encouragement that it needs to grow and ripen. Sacrifice is offered when the harvest is brought in, to thank the gods for seeing the people through another year. After a time it is assumed that the fertility of the soil depends on the sacrifices offered. No man would dare to break the cycle, for without the sacrifice the elements would turn hostile and the crops shrivel.

The endless cycle of seed-time and harvest, sowing and reaping, was the most amazing of all the mysteries of life. Every spring men threw seed into the ground. It was covered up, and, as far as they could see, it died. Then, with the warmth of the sun and the moisture of the rain, new life suddenly sprang out of the dark soil.

Before writing was invented men made up stories to illustrate this endless rhythm of existence. The most famous, which has come down to us through the Greeks, tells how Ceres, the mother goddess of the harvest, had a daughter called Persephone. Pluto, the god of the underworld, captured the girl and took her away to be queen of his dark kingdom. The mother was heartbroken to lose her girl, and at last she managed to strike a bargain with Pluto. For six months of the year the girl was to live with her husband in the underworld; then she would emerge into the sunshine and spend the other six months with her mother.

This is an early example of a religious *myth*—a story whose real meaning lies below the surface narrative. Persephone represents the seed, Pluto the dark soil, Ceres the Mother goddess who gives life to man. It was more than a story about the seasons and the harvest; it was a parable about all human life. The birth and death of the wheat seemed to mirror the cycle of man's own life, whereby one generation died and went into the ground, to be replaced by the next.

A child who asks the simple question 'Where did I come from?' has no knowledge of the anxieties and tensions which surround the subjects of sex and death in our modern society. Our ancestors treated the great moments of human existence without shame. The seed is sown, as a man and a woman come together in the sexual act. The new corn springs from the ground, as the child is born. The harvest time of life is when the old thankfully return to the earth from which they came. As Europeans travelled round the world in recent centuries, they were shocked to

Zulu wedding ceremony

find that in many places sexual acts and religious acts were looked on as one and the same thing. Yet the two have been linked together from the earliest times of man's religious experience. The erect male penis, the female breast and vagina, far from being unmentionable, feature in the religious art of many people as symbols of life and of creation. The life of man depends on the fertility of the human body, as it does on the fertility of the soil. Sexual actions were sometimes performed at autumn and spring festivals in the belief that they would encourage nature to follow the example set and bring a rich harvest.

As human communities became larger and more complex, so rules and regulations had to be laid down to govern the relationships within the community. Many of these regulations had clear reasons, and were designed, like all law, to see that one member of the community was not allowed to take advantage of another. Other customs grew up which did not have any immediately obvious relevance to everyday life, but which were just as strictly enforced as those which did. Certain actions became *tabu* (forbidden), and any offender against the regulations was severely punished. Some tabus are still very widespread, the most common of all being that which prohibits sexual intercourse between close relatives (incest). Biologists tell us that this deep instinct in man has helped to improve the quality of our species. Most tabus, however, differ from one tribe to another. The tabus have an important role to play in holding people of each tribe together in a single unit. Anyone who breaks the regulations is looked on as a danger to the whole people. His disobedience makes the gods angry and possibly may even render the sacrifices offered on behalf of the people ineffective. An offender generally has to submit to a process of cleansing to make himself fit to be brought back within the community again. At worst he might be driven out of the tribe altogether. To be cut off from the people, a homeless wanderer, at the mercy of the spirits is a worse fate than death itself.

Spirit worship of this sort is classified under the name of *animist* religion. There are many animists in different parts of the world today. It is a mistake, however, to assume that, because a religion is animist in nature, it is the same as that practised by primitive man. African religion, for instance, shows evidence of long development. It has, however, kept one thing in common with the religion of our early ancestors. Until very recently Africa has been a continent of very poor communications. The old tribal religions have not, therefore, been submitted to so much pressure from outside ideas and customs as would have been the case had people been able to move more freely. Lakes and groves of trees have kept their sacred significance from one generation to another. For generations an African has answered the question 'Who am I?' with the assertion 'I am an Ashanti', 'I am a Kikuyu'. His tribe provided him with a political and a religious structure of life. He gave it his loyalty and received in return a sense of belonging—of not being alone in a harsh and unknown world. But today, when there is much more movement of peoples within the continent, traditions of closely knit local units are quickly breaking down. As a man leaves his tribal area, so he leaves his tribal religion; he cannot easily adopt the gods and tabus of the people to whom he moves.

The great religions of the world, which still survive, with greater or lesser fortune, today, sprang up in areas where communications were easier. The two great homelands of religious thought were the river valleys of India and the Semitic countries of the Middle East. Before we turn to these two areas, however, we will look briefly at the particular contribution of a great race, who have been described as the least religious people on earth—the Chinese.

2
At One with Nature and the Community
TAOISM AND CONFUCIANISM

We have seen that 'primitive' religions are centred around two main themes. On the one hand, men wanted to be at one with the powerful forces of nature; on the other hand they needed to construct a system which would bind the community together in a coherent unit. These two features are present in most religions. In China, however, they were separated, and each formed the basis for separate systems which existed, for the most part peacefully, side by side. Both Taoism and Confucianism trace their origin to teachers who lived in the 6th Century B.C. The origins of both, however, stretch back much further into the earliest days of Chinese civilization.

TAOISM: MAN AND NATURE

It was said that the philosopher Lao Tzu worked in the court of the Emperor as keeper of the royal archives, but as time passed he grew more and more disgusted with the lives of the fashionable people about the throne. He therefore decided to withdraw himself completely so that he could live close to nature. Before he did so he wrote down his beliefs. Some 200 years later another philosopher, Chuang Tzu, continued his work and organized the religion which became known as Taoism.

The essence of the system put forward by Lao Tzu and Chuang Tzu was that men had to learn to live in unity with the great force of nature, which they called the *Tao*. Everything that was natural was good; everything that was unnatural was bad. Man had to get back to the time when he was a simple animal. Then, like other creatures, he could accept the round of life and death, happiness and

Lao-Tzu riding a water buffalo (National Palace Museum of the Rep. of China)

sorrow, pain and pleasure without complaint or anxiety. When Chuang Tzu 's wife died the philosopher sang a happy tune and beat time on a wooden bowl. Her death, he declared, represented but one more turn in the cycle of nature. Autumn had passed into winter; the leaf had fallen to become leaf mould.

The true men of old knew nothing of the love of life or of the hatred of death. Entrance into life occasioned them no joy; the exit from it awakened no resistance. Composedly they went and came. They did not forget what their beginning had been, and they did not enquire what their end would be. Thus there was in them the want of any mind to resist the Tao. Being such their minds were free from all thought; their demeanour was still and unmoved; their foreheads beamed simplicity. Whatever stillness came from others was like that of autumn; whatever warmth came from them was like that of spring. Their joy and anger assimilated to what we see in the four seasons.

The man who lived close to the Tao could have no more desire for fame and wealth than an animal. 'Keep life and lose those other things', advised the sage. Man had to learn to cut striving out of his life; to be content with the simple things which provide for the needs of a day-to-day existence. When living without Tao men always have to be doing something, reaching after something. The life of the striver is insecure since 'he who stands on tiptoe does not stand firm'. Those who possess the Tao, on the other hand, are able to do nothing, and be content. Even intellectual activity was regarded with suspicion.

If we could renounce our knowledge and discard our wisdom, it would be better for people a hundred fold. If we could renounce our benevolence and discard our morality, the people would again be dutiful and kindly. If we could renounce our skill and discard our scheming for gain, there would be no thieves nor robbers.

If men found such a life too plain, declared the sage, then they could feast their eyes on simplicity, and hold the Uncarved Block of stone in their hands. When they lived in unity with the Tao, nature would collaborate to make their life peaceful and happy. But when men broke with the natural order, they quickly brought all kinds of catastrophe—earthquake, flood and famine—on their own heads.

Ordinary people could not fully live out the Taoist philosophy. It did, however, provide a model which had great influence in shaping Chinese society. In her novel, *The Good Earth*, Pearl Buck described how Wang Lung, the farmer, grew old and tired. To give himself comfort he kept a coffin beside him in his room.

Spring passed and summer passed into harvest and in the hot autumn sun before winter comes Wang Lung sat where his father had sat against the wall. And he thought no more about anything now except his food and his drink and his land . . . And he was content holding it thus, and he thought of it fitfully and of his good coffin that was there, and the kind earth waited without haste until he came to it.

For the man who lived by Tao, nothing could be sudden or unexpected. Change was as slow as that brought about by water, dripping on a rock to wear it away. The old Chinese civilization had that same, timeless quality until the Europeans came and upset the Tao by digging canals, diverting rivers and sending belching steam engines careering across the countryside. They brought a doctrine of progress which directly contradicted everything which Lao Tzu and Chuang Tzu had taught. These old philosophers would hardly be happy about the fact that their countrymen have turned to follow the communist teachings of Karl Marx.

CONFUCIANISM: MAN AND SOCIETY

It is said that K'ung Fu Tzu (Confucius in western spelling) at one time met his contemporary Lao Tzu. The two men would certainly have had a certain amount in common. Like Lao Tzu, K'ung Fu Tzu left his official position, disgusted at the corruption of fashionable society. Unlike the Taoist, however, he did not try to retreat back to the

Discussing the Tao (National Palace Museum of the Rep. of China)

simplicity of nature, but, after years of wandering with his disciples, he set himself up as a teacher of good manners and morality.

K'ung Fu Tzu made no claim to be teaching anything new; indeed, he would have been shocked at the very idea. He believed that the people were straying from the path of true virtue, and he looked on it as his duty to bring them back. Unlike the Taoist teachers, he did not seek virtue in the simplicity of nature, but in the complex relationships between one man and his neighbour within society. His answer to the question, 'Who am I?' was therefore that every individual is a member of a community. Virtue lies in carrying out the duties which that community lays upon him. Unlike the Taoists, he had little interest in the great issues of existence, for

the path of duty lies in what is near and men seek for it in what is remote. The work of duty lies in what is easy and men seek for it in what is difficult.

K'ung Fu Tzu wrote out his instructions in large books, which have been the classics of Chinese education. He recorded the religious customs and court ceremonies which had been used for many generations, laid down the rules of behaviour for all and carefully rewrote the chronicles of ancient China. For more than 2,000 years Chinese students learnt his writings off by heart, in astonishing feats of memory, and it is sometimes difficult to see what benefit they could have gained from the exercise.

The real importance of K'ung Fu Tzu's work lay, not in the details of what he taught, but in the assumptions from which he worked, which were accepted as the basis of classical Chinese society. His whole system was based on a respect for authority. The simplest relationship, on which all others were based, was that between a son and his father. The son is inferior to his father, and so owes him respect and obedience. In return the father cares for and protects his son. In the same way, the wife is subordinate to her husband; the servant to his master. But a family consists not only of the living, but also of the dead. Every house had its shrine at which candles, wine and food were offered at the new moon and on other solemn occasions. Memorial days of ancestors were observed, and the dead members of the family were kept informed about all the great events—birth, marriage, sickness and death—of their descendants. A man had the duty of revering his dead ancestors, as he revered his living father. The structure of Chinese society was therefore founded on ancestor worship.

The rule which applied to the individual family unit applied also to the nation as a whole. The Emperor, as the father of all his people, deserved the highest level of respect. He presided at the Celestial Court where he received honour due to a divine rather than a human figure. His responsibilities were proportionately great, since he was held responsible not only for human concerns like the preservation of law and order, but also for averting natural calamities, such as floods and storms.

(opposite) *A Literary Gathering. The Scholar was held in the highest regard in Confucian society (National Palace Museum of the Rep. of China)*

Under the Emperor, society was arranged in an elaborate pyramid, arranged not by birth, but by virtue.

The Scholar At the top of the pyramid was the learned man who had studied deeply and passed searching examinations in the Confucian classics and other ancient works. His life was supposed to be a model of virtue.
The Farmer Next in honour came the farmer, by whose labour the necessities of life were produced from the earth.
The Artisan took a lower place than the farmer because he fashioned the raw materials which other people had produced.
The Merchant rated lower still because both the farmer and the artisan contributed to making the objects which they bought and sold.
The Soldier rated lowest of all—a virtual outcast from society—because his task in life was to destroy what others had made.

It is interesting to note that this order of precedence in society is almost the opposite of that which has for centuries been taken for granted in the West.

True virtue consisted in giving the other person, be he higher or lower in the social scale, the respect due to him. 'What is human-heartedness?' asked a pupil. The master K'ung Fu Tzu replied by expounding the 'golden rule' of behaviour.

In public behave as you would in the presence of an honoured guest. Set the people their public tasks as if you were conducting a great sacrifice. The treatment you would not have for yourself, do not hand out to others. Then there will be no resentment against you in the state, no resentment in your clan.

On another occasion he advised,

The man of honour makes demands on himself: the man without a sense of honour makes demands on others.

It has been said that Confucianism cannot be called a religion, because it is only concerned with man and society. 'Why do you ask me about death,' said the Master, 'when you do not know how to live?' In a Confucian temple a worshipper communes, not with God, but with his ancestors. A man's survival after death depends on the sons which he bears who will continue to do him honour, as he did honour to those who went before him. Even though it lacks some of the elements of what is generally called 'religion', Confucianism is a sincere attempt to find an answer to the question, 'Who am I?' Man can only find his true self, replies the Master, when he lives dutifully as a part of an unchanging society.

During the course of our own century Chinese society has, of course, undergone immense upheavals, which have torn apart the classical Confucian structure. But something of the old remains. The traditional respect for the cultivator of the soil has fitted well with the doctrines of communism. Most remarkable, however, is the way in which respect for authority has survived revolution. The Celestial Emperor was more than a human being; he was a god on earth. Even after accepting the doctrines of Karl Marx, the Chinese people still seem to need to treat their ruler as more than human. Chairman Mao remains the father of his people; the apex of loyalty which holds an immense people together. His Thoughts have become a sacred book of our own time. As Alice found when she was in Wonderland, even when the Cheshire Cat disappears, its smile lingers on.

3
Thou Art That
HINDUISM

2,000 years before the time of Lao Tzu and K'ung Fu Tzu
a civilization had flourished around the rivers of north
India. In recent years archaeologists have worked among the
ruins of the cities built by people that have been called the
Dravidians. Tablets with writing on them have been found,
but so far no one has been able to decipher them and so
our knowledge of these early town dwellers is limited to
what can be pieced together from their buildings and their
art.

Probably at some time during the 2nd millennium
B.C.—there is disagreement about the date—invaders with a
more primitive culture, but better weapons, crossed the
mountains from the north and defeated the Dravidians.
These warriors, who were of the same racial stock as
Europeans, have been called the *Aryans*. They did not
destroy everything that they found in their path, but
gradually mingled with the Dravidians and the more
primitive tribes which had lived in the sub-continent for
even longer than the Dravidians. Out of this coming
together of different peoples was born the religion of
Hinduism, which took its name from the great river Indus.

Scholars have tried to disentangle the specifically
Dravidian and the specifically Aryan threads, which have,
over the centuries, become woven together into this rich
and varied religion.

Dravidian Religion
It seems clear from archaeological remains that worship in
the ancient cities was based on the idea of fertility, (see
pages 7-8). Statues of both male and female deities have
been dug up, on which the sexual organs are exaggerated.

Aryan Religion

We know more about Aryan religion because their chants were handed down by word of mouth from master to student over many centuries before being written down in the world's oldest sacred books, which are known as the *Vedas*. The Aryans disapproved of the sexual element in Dravidian religion, and directed their worship at gods which represented the powerful forces of nature. Their view of the world had much in common with that found in the Greek myths. Heaven was the abode of the gods who represented the sun and the moon, night and dawn, storm and fire. The middle region of the earth was peopled by men. Below there was an underworld, inhabited by the shades of the dead. These warrior people appear to have met to perform their sacrifices around a fire in the open air. There they sang their hymns, like this one to Night, who is seen as a being with many eyes.

Night drawing near has looked abroad,
In many places with her eyes;
All glories has she now assumed.

Pervaded has the immortal one
The depths, the heights, the ample space;
With light she drives away the gloom.

The goddess Night approaching nigh,
Her sister Dawn has ousted quite;
Her darkness too will disappear.

To us this day thou has appeared,
At whose approach we see our homes
As birds their nests upon the tree.

Home too have gone the villagers,
Home those possessing feet and wings,
Home even the greedy hawks have gone.

Ward off the she-wolf and the wolf,
Ward off the thief, O brooding Night.
And be so easy to traverse.

Regular performance of the sacrifices kept the people in harmony with the powerful forces of nature. If they ceased to be carried out, then human life would become impossible in a hostile world. The priests who performed the rituals had to learn the words and the actions with absolute precision. The smallest slip could make the whole sacrifice worthless and plunge the people into misery.

THE INDIAN WORLD VIEW

When two different peoples come into contact with each other one of two things will happen; either the stronger will destroy the weaker or the two cultures will merge. There was certainly killing and violence in the early days of the invasion, but the older ways of thought were not destroyed. Gradually the different racial groups learnt to share the same land. By developing the *caste system* (see pages 36-8) they kept themselves in some measure apart, but their religions gradually merged. Many new ideas were introduced into the Aryan Vedic beliefs.

The Hindu world view which emerged from this mixture of ideas is quite different from that held in the West. It therefore takes some effort for a European to understand it. Nearly all people in the world have asked the question, 'How did the world come into existence?' Scientists are still not agreed on any single explanation. Primitive people made up myths to explain how things began. The myth in the Rig Veda, oldest of the Vedas, is much more complicated than the one in Genesis, which Westerners know better.

Then neither Being nor Not-Being existed, neither air, nor the heaven, nor what is above it. What did it encompass? Where? In whose protection? What was water, the deep, unfathomable. Neither death nor immortality was there then, no sign of night or day . . . In the beginning was darkness swathed in darkness: all this was but unmanifested water. Whatever was . . . was generated by the power of heat. In the beginning desire which was the first seed of mind overcovered it.

It is clear that the old priests who composed this myth were not trying to *give an account* of the beginning of the world, but to *interpret* it. Two points should be noted.

a) The universe was created by the action of heat upon the emptiness, which is called the *void*.

b) The first awakening of the human mind came from the sensation of desire.

In the Genesis narrative the Bible tells us that God looked out on his handiwork 'and saw that it was very good'. Hindus would not agree with this verdict. To them the world is not very good; quite the reverse, it is a place of trouble and suffering.

Those who have been brought up in the West think of time as continuing on a straight line. Hindus think of time as going round and round in vast and endless circles. This was probably a Dravidian contribution to the religion, as there is no sign of any such belief in the early Vedas. The cycle of day and night is repeated on an immense scale of cosmic time. For 12,000,000 years the world is in daylight; for another 12,000,000 years it is in night. The 24,000,000 years together form but a single day to Brahmah, the Great Creator.

Man is caught up in this endless process by the desires which have called his life into being. He spends his existence desperately striving for the things which he thinks will bring him pleasure, but all the time he is only strapping himself ever more firmly onto the wheel of existence. This process is called *samsara*—wandering. Even death does not bring escape, for man dies only to be reborn again and again. The condition of his new birth is set by the actions of his previous lives. If he lives virtuously, he will be reborn into a higher caste. If he is disobedient, he will plunge downward to be reborn out of the womb of an outcaste, or of some unclean animal. He might even become an insect or at worst be denied a body altogether and drift helplessly, a 'hungry ghost' through the vast empty spaces of time.

Those who have been brought up within the Western tradition are accustomed to look upon the world as something very solid and real. To the Hindu, on the other hand, that world of objects is an illusion. The only difference between the world about us and a dream is that the dream exists in the mind of just one man, while the world is a fantasy shared by all men at the same time. One Hindu thinker compared the universe to a piece of rope lying on the ground. Someone approaching sees it and mistakes it for a snake. In that man's mind at that moment the rope is a snake. In the same way the world appears real to our minds. But in fact there is only one reality and that is the Supreme Essence, which lies in all things. This Supreme Essence, or *Brahman*, we may call God.

THE HINDU VIEW OF GOD

Hinduism is probably the most tolerant religion on earth. Born out of a marriage between Dravidian and Aryan beliefs, it spread outwards to other people in the Indian sub-continent. But no one had to 'be converted' to a new set of beliefs, by putting aside his old gods. Fertility cults continued to be practised alongside the more severe Vedic sacrifices.

Hindus are therefore in one sense *polytheists* (people who worship many gods). From very early times, however, some began to see the many gods as but different faces of a single God. 'Though men call it by many names,' said the Rig Veda, 'it is really One.' A later teacher explained the great variety of gods to an early European visitor.

We have indeed in our temples a great variety of images. To all these images we pay great honour; prostrating our bodies, and presenting to them, with much ceremony, flowers, rice, scented oil, saffron, and other similar articles. Yet we do not believe that these statues are themselves Brahma or Vishnu; but merely their images and representations. We show them deference only for the sake of the deity whom they represent, and when we pray it is not to the statue, but to that deity. Images are admitted in our temples, because we conceive that prayers are offered up with more devotion where there is something before the eyes that fixes the mind; but in fact we acknowledge that God alone is absolute, that He only is the omnipotent Lord.

We may take it that this is the educated man's view of

God. Simple worshippers in the temple do not always think in such large, abstract terms. To be a Hindu there is no need to believe in one God, or in many gods, or indeed in any god at all. Hindus have spent many centuries in arguing about the nature of God, but they have never felt strongly enough about the matter to persecute those who did not agree with them. It is therefore impossible to define what Hindus as a whole believe by the word *God*. It is, however, possible to say that the word means something very different in India from what it does in the West.

To start to understand the difference in which people of the two cultures look on *God*, we must first understand that there is a profound difference in the way in which they look on *man*. In the West he is seen as a creature set apart from the rest of the animal kingdom. We will see (page 76) that this is clearly stated in the Genesis creation story, and western people have accepted this assumption ever since. Indians have always looked on man as being just a part of the whole animal kingdom. Indeed a man's soul might be reborn into the body of an animal, a bird, fish or insect. The Indian therefore feels a much stronger sense of unity with nature than is common among westerners. When he looks for God, he is not therefore projecting the idea of a *person* like a man only rather larger, such as western artists have portrayed. He is looking instead for a spirit or essence which binds nature together. One school of Hindu thought goes the whole way to the point of view which is known as *pantheism* and says that God not only is everywhere, but *is everything*. God is like salt dissolved in water. The water and the salt are one; it cannot be seen or separated. But its taste is everywhere; it pervades everything. The Veda expresses the idea in abstract form.

The soul of all creatures is one soul, but it is also present in every creature; unity and plurality at the same time, like the reflection of the moon on the water.

A father tried to put the same idea in more concrete terms so that his son would be able to understand.

When Svetaketu, at his father's bidding, had brought a ripe fruit from the banyam tree, his father said to him,
'Split the fruit in two, dear son.'
'Here you are. I have split it in two.'
'What do you find there?'
'Innumerable tiny seeds.'
'Then take one of the seeds and split it.'
'I have split the seed.'
'And what do you find there?'
'Why, nothing, nothing at all.'
'Ah, dear son, but this great tree cannot possibly come from nothing. Even if you cannot see with your eyes that subtle something in the seed which produces this mighty form, it is present nonetheless, that is the power, that is the spirit unseen, which pervades everywhere and is all things. Have faith! That is the spirit which lies at the root of all existence, and that also art thou, O Svetaketu.'

There can be no more extreme statement of the unity between man and nature. The subtle something which is in the seed, is in every created thing; the power which makes the tree grow; the spirit unseen which is in all things—that is God. God is not *in* the tree—God *is* the tree. Man is bound up in the same power. THOU ART THAT. The father is saying to his son that God is not merely *in* him—God *is* him.

It is said that an Indian sage once cried out in joy, 'I am food; I am food.' He had reached the stage when he felt that his own personality was completely lost in the world of nature. All creatures eat and are eaten. Man also eats, and must give himself to be eaten. Once he has reached that understanding, the wheel of samsara no longer has any power over him because all of his old desires have melted away. Liberation is near.

THE HINDU WAY OF LIFE

Travellers from the West have noted that there is a hint of sadness in the Indian make-up. The Hindu might comment in his turn that this should cause no surprise since, with

A couple of beggar priests in a street in Calcutta

suffering and pain all around, the world is a sad place in which to live. Despite this, however, it would most certainly not be true to say that the Hindu is particularly prone to anxiety or despair. His religion provides him with well charted routes to follow as he travels through the world of illusion and suffering. In his search for liberation he can choose to follow any one of three paths—or any combination of the three. They are the Way of Devotion, the Way of Works and the Way of Yoga. At the end of the road, when he comes near to his destination, lies the ultimate Way of Understanding.

The Way of Devotion

Hinduism has not cut itself away from its old polytheistic
roots. We have seen that in primitive religions certain
places are set aside as specially holy or the spirit of the
gods is said to reside in particular animals. As Hinduism
embraced the older religions of India, no one was asked to
give up his traditional ways of worship. Millions gather on
holy days to wash themselves in the sacred waters of the
river Ganges. The cow is still protected from being
slaughtered and is worshipped as a sacred animal—perhaps
as a reminder of the days when the Aryan tribesmen
herded cattle on the wide plains to the north of the
Himalayas.

Learned scholars argue as to whether God is one, and
whether he is in everything, as the old story said. Simple
peasants take little interest in such speculation, but pour
out their religious feelings in the ceremonies which take
place in the local temples. They do not ask what God is
like—they just lavish all their love on the particular deity
of their choice.

Hinduism has a multitude of gods. Some came from the
Dravidians, some from the Aryans, some from other
peoples absorbed into the Hindu fold. Over the centuries
they have merged and acquired new personalities until
three, Brahma, Vishnu and Siva, emerged supreme. Westerners, trying to find parallels with Christianity, have called
these three the Hindu Trinity (see page 116)—Brahma, the
Creator, Vishnu the Preserver, Siva the Destroyer. In fact
these three gods do not have such neatly defined roles.
Also, while the Christian worships all three members of his
Trinity, the Hindu will choose only one of these gods as
the object of his devotion.

Brahma. It is easy to become confused with three
different words which use the same root. Brahman is the
word used for the supreme essence of life; that which is
there when the seed is split. It is therefore the word which
might be translated as God (with a capital G). A brahmin is
a human being who is a member of the priestly caste (see
page 36). Brahma is the least popular of the three supreme

19th Century Hindu painting of the four-headed Goddess, Durga,
here seen as a destroying force

gods, and only one temple is now dedicated to his worship in the whole of India.

Vishnu. This, the most attractive of Hindu gods, commands immense devotion from followers of his cult in many parts of India—and, indeed, his influence is spreading even in the Western world through the Hare Krishna movement. The ancient stories tell how Vishnu took on human form at different times to live with and talk to men. The most famous of these *manifestations* was when he took the form of the charioteer Krishna who fought on the winning side in one of the most bloody battles of all literature. The book called *The Bhagavad-Gita* tells of the advice which he gave to his chosen friend Arjuna before the battle. At the end of the book he binds his worshipper to his service.

And now again give ear to this my all-highest word,
Of all the most mysterious:
'I love thee well.'
Therefore will I tell thee thy salvation.

Bear me in mind, love me and worship me,
Sacrifice, prostrate thyself to me:
So shalt thou come to me, I promise thee
Truly, for thou art dear to me.

Give up all things of law,
Turn to me, thine only refuge,
I will deliver thee
From all evils; have no care . . .

But whoever shall proclaim this all-highest mystery
To my loving devotees
Showing the while the highest love and loyalty to me,
Shall come to me in very truth.

Krishna not only appears as a warrior, but also as the ideal lover. Another story tells how in one incarnation he was brought up as a child in the home of a peasant to preserve him from a wicked king. He grew to be such a beautiful young man that all the girls who herded cows, and were called gopis, fell in love with him. Indian artists loved to carve Krishna with his devoted gopis, and particularly with the lucky girl who was picked out for his special attentions. The theme of love runs strongly through the Vishnu cults. As a man loves a woman, so God loves human beings. But the humans, like the gopis, can only wait and hope that the god will deign to come to them. The god is male—the active force; the worshipper is female—passive and waiting.

The Vishnu festivals are among the most popular and lively in India. One of the most famous is at Puri where the immense Jagaunath is pulled out through the streets on a wooden cart. The Jagaunath, which is dressed all over in splendid clothes, is supposed to be a manifestation of Krishna himself, and stories, which are probably much exaggerated, have been told of how frenzied worshippers have thrown themselves onto the ground to be crushed beneath the wheels of the cart.

Siva. If one of the three gods is to be counted supreme, it must be Siva, who appears linked with his wife Parvati or Kali. If Vishnu represents the power of love, Siva personifies power itself—the activity which keeps the world in existence. He is both gentle and terrible, creator and destroyer. Siva dances with wild joy, and the world comes into existence; he dances with mad frenzy and all is destroyed again. Thus he represents the cycle of life and death which builds up into the endless rhythm of time.

From the Dravidians comes the ancient sexual symbolism of creation. In the very holiest place in Siva's temple stands the phallus (see page 7) which is his symbol. Yet, although he represents the force of sexual energy, the god and his goddess are always pure.

The devotee of Siva looks on the two faces of the god and his consort with equal devotion. Parvati is beauty itself, the symbol of the devotion a wife should have for her husband. Yet, as Kali, she can become one of the most fearful deities ever worshipped by man.

Ever art thou dancing in battle, Mother. Never was beauty like thine, as, with thy hair flowing about thee, thou dost ever dance, a naked warrior on the breast of Siva.

Parvati, the consort of Siva, is beauty itself

Government of India Tour

Heads of thy sons, daily fresh killed, hang as a garland around thy neck. How is thy waist adorned with human hands! Little children are thy ear-rings. Faultless are thy lovely lips; thy teeth are fair as the jasmine in full bloom. Thy face is bright as the lotus flower, and terrible is its constant smiling. Beautiful as the rain clouds is thy form: all blood-stained are thy feet.

Prasad says: My mind is as one that dances. No longer can my eyes behold such beauty.

In Siva the opposites come together. The 'madman with the moon-crowned hair' is at the same time the source of life and joy. The male and the female principles are brought together as the foundation of the power of nature. As a Sivite poet wrote,

Once I went to Aiyaru, with light and reverent tread,
I saw come two young elephants, male by loved female led,
And in that sight I saw God's foot, saw secret things unsaid.

The opposing aspects of Siva's and Parvati's personalities do not represent good and bad; they are the basic principles of energy which are bound up in the bundle of existence.

Over the centuries a number of 'left hand' Sivite groups have concentrated on the destructive side of the cult. The great majority of his worshippers, however, hold the two

Government of India Tourist Office

A panel from the temple at Khajuraho, showing the link between religion and erotic love

together. Although the sexual element is strongly empha-
sised in the cult, the followers of Siva generally live by a
stricter code of conduct than do those of the more gentle
Vishnu. The devotee finds all his fulfillment in the act of
worship of his chosen god.

Why fast and starve, why suffer pains austere?
Why climb the mountains doing penance harsh?

Why go to bathe in waters far and near?
Release is theirs, and theirs alone, who call
At every time upon the Lord of all.

Educated Hindus are sometimes embarrassed by the cults which help worshippers along the way of devotion. They feel that they have to apologise for the simplicity of some of the practices, for the priests who tend idols as if they were human—washing them, feeding and clothing them. But for the masses of Hindus, especially those of low caste, the path of devotion is simple and within their grasp. It also brings joy and colour into their lives.

The Way of Works and Duty

We have seen (page 23) that the condition in which a person was destined to be reborn was set by the way in which he performed the duties laid on him in life. This is the least spectacular of the three ways, but it is of great importance to the whole Hindu way of life. Every person in society had duties laid on him, and virtue lies in performing these duties diligently and without complaint.

In the Western world we have always assumed that a good man is a man who does virtuous acts. It is therefore easier for us to understand the way of works than other aspects of Hinduism. Krishna, the charioteer, explained this path to his young companion in the Bhagavad-Gita.

Work alone is thy proper business,
Never the fruits it may produce.

It is therefore of no value for anyone to put great effort into following the way of works if all the time he is really striving for the financial rewards or even the 'good name' he will win from his exertions. In the Bhagavad-Gita Krishna exclaims, 'How pitiful are they whose motive is the fruit of works.' The main criticism that Hindus would make of Western men and women is that we are obsessed with striving after the fruit of our works.

A family performing Delvali

Hindus believe that they must follow the course of duty in all aspects of life. They lay great stress on the responsibilities placed upon father, mother and children within the family. It is part of a man's religious duty to set up a household and care for his wife and children. It is right for him to strive for material wealth so that he can give those who are dependent on him the good things of life. The woman's role is to live and care for her husband. The female's position is subordinate to that of the male, and, indeed, some have gone so far as to say that, once a woman is married, she has no real existence outside that of her husband. For many centuries it was considered right for a *sati* (a real and true woman) to sacrifice her own life when her husband died by throwing herself onto his funeral pyre. Observers remarked how women killed themselves in this way with expressions of rapt devotion on their faces. The child's duty is to obey his or her parents. The young person respects the father's wishes, even when it comes to choosing a husband or wife.

Beyond the general duties laid on all males and females, every individual has had special duties laid upon him according to the *caste* into which he was born. The origin of the caste system lies back in the time of the Aryan invasions. The Aryans may well have had their own society divided between priests, warriors and peasants. Out of the mixture of the peoples came the four basic castes of Hindu society. The first three were the *twice born*, who could participate in the sacrifices and learn the wisdom of the Vedas. In order of rank, they were,

Brahmins—priests.
Kshatrayas—warriors.
Vaisyas—farmers and traders.

Below them came the *once born* common folk,

Sudras—peasants.

Every man had a special role to fulful within the appointed order, and he was certainly not fulfilling his duty if he tried to climb to the ranks of a higher caste. Although some cases of inter-marriage are recorded, it was generally looked upon as very undesirable. Indeed one of the main signs of the end of one of the world's ages, when everything was slipping to destruction, was that members of different castes would forget their place and mix one with the other.

To the priestly caste were entrusted the mysteries of the ancient sacrifices. The Brahmin was revered, almost as a god. His duty was not to gather wealth for himself—as has been the custom of the 'upper classes' in most societies—but to use his position for the benefit of all the people.

When a Brahmin is born he is born superior to the whole earth, he is the lord of all creatures, and he has to guard the treasury of religion. Everything that exists throughout the world is the private property of the Brahmin. By the high excellence of his birth he is entitled to everything.

The task of government was left to the kings and princes, who were drawn from the warrior caste. A king's sacred duty was to extend the frontiers of his kingdom, and leave it more powerful than he had found it. The warrior's duty was to make war, as it was the farmer's to till the land and the merchant's to carry on his trade. The sudra had to find his contentment in serving others.

Outside the caste system altogether there was another large group, the *outcastes*, or untouchables, who had no place at all in the order of things. Since it was assumed that they had brought their fate upon themselves by the wickedness of their early lives, few caste Hindus felt compassion for their lot. The outcaste, being unclean, was given all the filthy and degrading jobs to do.

In time the division of Hindu society became much more complex, and the four basic groups subdivided further into over 2,000 different castes. Many of these were occupational groupings, like the guilds of medieval Europe. A father handed on his skill to his son, who in turn married within the little community. Each caste was largely self-governing, laying down the regulations for trade and the religious duties of the members. These rigid dividing lines between different groups of people prevented Indian society from developing as rapidly as that of Europe, where people were able to move more easily between one social group and another.

Even in the early days men began to face up to serious problems when they felt that their *caste* duty came into conflict with their *moral* duty. This is vividly illustrated in the Bhagavad-Gita. Yudhishtira, the rightful king of the land, had been ousted from his inheritance by his relatives. He had no longing for power, and would have accepted any compromise which would have preserved his honour, but his enemies refused to come to any settlement so that in the end, following his caste duty, he drew up an army to regain his kingdom. In his own heart, however, he was unhappy. The kingdom which was rightfully his could not, he felt, be worth so many lives.

Yudhishtira's brother Arjuna, looked out over the field where the armies were drawn up and confessed his sorrow to his friend, the charioteer, Krishna.

and Arjuna beheld
fathers, grandsires,

Venerable teachers, uncles, brothers, sons,
Grandsons and comrades.

Fathers-in-law and friends
Standing there in either host.
And the son of Kunti, seeing them,
All his kinsmen thus arrayed,

Was filled with deep compassion
And, desponding, spake these words:
'Krishna, when these mine own folk I see
Standing, spoiling for the fight,

My limbs give way
My mouth dries up, and trembling
Takes hold upon my frame:
My body's hairs stand up in dread.

My bow, Gandiva, slips from my hand,
My very skin is all ablaze;
I cannot stand, my mind
Seems to wander, all distraught.

But the charioteer will not let him shirk the duty which
fate laid upon him.

Consider thine own caste duty,
Then too thou hast no cause to quail;
For better than a fight prescribed by duty
Is nothing for a man of princely class . . .

But if thou wilt not wage this war
Prescribed by thy caste duty,
Then by casting off both honour and caste duty,
Thou wilt bring evil on thyself.

The clash between moral duty and caste duty was acted
out in real life by the 20th century saint and political
leader, Mahatma Gandhi. Born a caste Hindu, he started
early to question whether the treatment of untouchables
was morally right. For the sake of what he considered the
higher duty of compassion, he broke caste regulations by
befriending and caring for those people who he called
Harijans (people of God). As leader of the Indian nation
struggle against British rule Gandhi insisted that his
followers should abide by the principle of non-violence

which he understood as being the true duty of the Hindu people. Even when Moslems and Hindus were killing one another, he continued to insist that lasting solutions to the problems of his country could only be found in love and unity. Many traditional Hindus felt that he was betraying the cause of his own people, and at the end of his long and incredibly fruitful life he was killed by a Hindu fanatic.

Today there remains deep division of opinion among Hindus as to where the path of duty lies. Many continue to see it in terms of the traditional caste duty, and oppose all change in the old order. Those who have taken their lead from Gandhi, on the other hand, believe that India has a new duty to show the world that life can be lived without violence, and with compassion for all creatures.

The Way of Yoga or Union

We have seen that man became trapped in the endless cycle of existence by the birth of his desire (page 23). He may improve his position in the pyramid of existence by carrying out his duty faithfully, but in the end, if he would reach the state of oneness with Brahman, he must embark on the hard discipline which leads to the quelling of desire and the finding of the true self. According to the Bhagavad-Gita, even on the day of batle, Krishna, the charioteer, pointed his young companion to this way that leads to peace. For the man who does not know peace, says the god, there can be no joy. His senses rove hither and thither, like a ship, tossed in the sea. But the wise man is still and calm.

In what for all other folk is night,
Therein the man of self restraint is wide awake.
What time all other folk are awake,
That time is night for the sage who sees.

As the waters flow in to the sea,
Full filled, unmoving in its depths,
So too do all desires flow into the heart of man:
And such a man wins peace,—not the desirer of desires.

The man who puts off all desires
And roams around from longing freed,

Who does not think, 'This I am,' or 'This is mine,'
Draws near to peace.

No man is under any obligation to set out on the hard
road of discipline, known as *yoga*. If he feels he is not
ready in his current life, he can die and be born again,
when he will have another chance. A man may turn to
yoga when he is young and spend a lifetime seeking the
peace that Krishna describes; or he may fulfil his duty by
raising a family and carrying out the business of life until
he is old, and then go into the forest to discipline his body
and mind.

Some have looked for this fulfilment of their life in
solitude, but the traditional Hindu way is for the seeker to
attach himself to a *guru* (teacher) who is experienced
enough to show him the way. The yogi has to cut himself
free from all those emotions which keep him on the wheel
of desire. To achieve this he has to bring his body under
strict control.

The yoga exercises, worked out by gurus down the
centuries, are becoming popular in the West, for they have
proved effective in relieving the strains and stresses of
modern life. European exercises are traditionally designed
to make the muscles of the body stronger. The yogi is not
interested in improving his muscular power, but only in
bringing his body under complete control, so that it no
longer gets in the way of the greater task of controlling the
mind. He adopts a position of the body in which he can
remain still for long periods and does exercises designed to
help him establish complete mastery over the mechanical
process of breathing. He uses his voice, repeating over and
over again the long syllable 'Om'. This ancient practice was
recommended by Krishna in the Bhagavad-Gita, when he
advises the yogi:

Let him utter the word Om, Brahman in one syllable,
Keeping me in mind.

The word starts loudly, then trails away into silence.

Some of the yoga exercises release astonishing powers of
the body, and many travellers in India have described how

they have seen Indian holy men perform seemingly impossible feats. It is always stressed that the beginner must practice under the supervision of a guru, or he may do harm to himself.

The physical exercises are but a preparation for the true purpose of yoga, which consists in bringing the mind under control through the processes of concentration, meditation and contemplation.

Concentration. It is first necessary to clear the mind of all those flitting images which normally occupy it by pinning it down to a single object. The nature of the object itself does not matter; it is only important that it should fill the mind to the exclusion of everything else.

Meditation. The yogi then goes on to broaden out from the act of concentration to consider the object in its wider relationship to other things. The lily floats on the water—the water and the lily are brought together to become one.

Contemplation. The final stage comes when the yogi has lost himself in contemplation. This is a state of joy which comes on suddenly. The brain is free from desire and the yogi can catch a glimpse of that true essence which is in all things.

The path takes discipline and patience, but the understanding which leads to nirvana cannot be achieved by striving after it, for striving is itself desire. Nor is it achieved by activity of the intellect—what westerners described as 'thinking'—for the brain has to become completely still. By following the path of yoga the devotee has sought the true Self which lies within himself.

Yoga provides the discipline which opens the human being up to the stillness of meditation and the joy of contemplation. The devotee of Vishnu or Siva will prepare himself for the great festivals of his god by the ancient physical and mental exercises. Yoga provides the pathway to the highest experiences of the Hindu's life.

The Way of Understanding
The three Ways which we have studied lead in one direction. The worshipper seeks that oneness which the Hindu understands as God. 'Split the seed,' said the father. 'There is Brahman, the Supreme Essence of life. "Thou art That".'

In the final way the Hindu tries to understand the oneness of all life. He seeks a knowledge, which is not just cluttering the mind with facts, but a deep insight which cuts to the heart of all existence. When he reaches this understanding he becomes like a drop of water entering a great ocean. His own soul—the tiny drop—is not obliterated, for the ocean has joined the drop as much as the drop has joined the ocean. For many lives he has prepared, following faithfully along the three lower ways. Now the desires which kept him on the wheel of existence fall away as he becomes at one with Brahman.

This is the fixed, still state of Brahman;
He who wins through to this is nevermore perplexed.
Standing therein at the time of death
To the Nirvana that is Brahman too he goes!

4
There is no Self

BUDDHISM

A king once asked a question of a wise man. "Why are men not all alike? Why do some have a long or short life, some health or illness, beauty or ugliness, courage or cowardice?"

The wise man asked in return. "Why do not all plants resemble each other? Why, according to their species, are they sour or salty, bitter or acid, astringent or sweet?"

"Because of the difference in their seeds."

"So do men differ according to the diversity of their acts which, like seeds of themselves, they have planted in former lives."

THE BIRTH AND CHILDHOOD OF GAUTAMA BUDDHA

In about the year 567 B.C. a son was born to a king who ruled in South Nepal. The child, whose name was Siddhartha Gautama, was destined to become one of the three great religious figures in the history of the world, known and revered as the Buddha, the Enlightened One. At the time that he lived there were no books in India, so the story of his life was not written down for another 400 years. By the time that it was put on paper, history had become mixed up with legend.

As with Jesus and Mahommed, the stories show him as having been a very remarkable child. One account tells how immediately after he was born he walked seven steps in each of four directions, and a lotus flower bloomed in each of his footprints. Most Buddhists do not worry whether such stories are historically accurate or not. They do, however, assert that the young Gautama was both physically and morally a model of what a human being

The bronze Buddha inside the Marble Temple, Bangkok

should be. This was, however, no accident, for the child had lived through many previous existences. In each of these he had moved closer and closer to that state of perfection he achieved in this, his final appearance on earth. The seed was good and the plant grew straight and true.

The king was very proud of his son, and hoped that he would grow to carry out his duty as a member of the warrior caste by becoming a powerful and successful ruler. But he was very worried by the prophecy of a holy man who said that the lad might turn away from worldly concerns and follow the spiritual path to become a great religious leader. He determined therefore that his son should be brought up in a manner suitable for a prince. He surrounded him with handsome companions of his own age, and gave him everything that he could possibly want. Gautama grew up to be a fine, handsome lad, quick to learn and popular with everybody. When old enough to marry he was given the beautiful and pure Yashodhara as his bride.

In course of time the fair-bosomed Yashodhara bore . . . a son, who was named Rahula. It must be remembered that all those who will attain enlightenment, must first of all know the taste of the pleasures which the senses can give. Only then, after a son has been born to them, do they depart into the forest.

His Withdrawal

Fearing that Gautama might well go off to seek the path of enlightenment rather than stay to rule the kingdom which he would inherit, the king tried to make sure that nothing should come into his son's life which could possibly induce him to take such a course. His companions were to keep his mind on the pleasures of life and they had particular instructions that on no account should the young man see anything of human pain or sorrow.

But the bitter side of life could not be shut off from the boy's view for ever.

In the course of time the women told him how much they loved the groves near the city, and how delightful they were. So, feeling like an elephant locked up inside a house, he set his heart on making a journey outside the palace. The king heard of the plans of his dearly beloved son, and arranged a pleasure excursion which would be worthy of his own affection and royal dignity, as well as of his son's youth. But he gave orders that all the common folk with any kind of affliction should be kept away from the royal road, because he feared that they might agitate the prince's sensitive mind. Very gently all cripples were driven away, and all those who were crazy, aged, ailing, and the like, and also all wretched beggars. So the royal highway became supremely magnificent.

The citizens jubilantly acclaimed the prince. But the Gods of the Pure Abode, when they saw that everyone was happy as if in Paradise, conjured up the illusion of an old man, so as to induce the king's son to leave his home. The prince's charioteer explained to him the meaning of old age. The prince reacted to this news like a bull when a lightning-flash crashes down near him. For his understanding was purified by the noble intentions he had formed in his past lives and by the good deeds he had accumulated over countless aeons. In consequence his lofty soul was shocked to hear of old age. He sighed deeply, shook his head, fixed his gaze on the old man, surveyed the festive multitude, and, deeply perturbed, said to the charioteer: 'So that is how old age destroys indiscriminately the memory, beauty, and strength of all! And yet with such a sight before it the world goes on quite unperturbed. This being so, my son, turn round the horses, and travel back quickly to our palace! How can I delight to walk about in parks when my heart is full of fear of ageing?' So at the bidding of his master's son the charioteer reversed the chariot.

On his second journey out of the palace he saw a man with a diseased body. On his third he saw a corpse; leaning on the chariot rail he called out,

This is the end which has been fixed for all, and yet the world forgets its fears and takes no heed! The hearts of men are surely hardened unto fears, for they feel quite at ease while travelling along the road to the next life. Turn back the chariot! This is no time or place for pleasure excursions. How could an intelligent person pay no heed at the time of disaster, when he knows of his impending destruction.

From that time onwards Gautama withdrew himself

from the pleasures of the court. Finally, on his 29th birthday, he watched sadly as his companions celebrated and drank themselves to sleep. When at last they had all settled for the night he went into Yashodhara's room, and looked down tenderly at his sleeping wife and child. Then he called his charioteer and set out into the night. Once away from the palace, he cut off his long aristocratic hair with his sword, changed clothes with a beggar and walked into the forest.

The Enlightenment

Siddhartha Gautama had been born and brought up as a Hindu. He therefore sought for liberation by following the path of yoga (pages 39-42). He went in turn to two gurus, and learnt all that they could teach, but at the end he was still dissatisfied. He then attached himself to five other seekers and together they practised the *ascetic* way of life. Sometimes he ate no more than a single grain of rice; sometimes he remained standing for days on end until he wore his body to a living skeleton. But still he could find no satisfaction. Realizing at last that he would achieve nothing by such methods, he accepted a bowl of curds from a milkmaid. This so disgusted his five companions that they went off and left him.

Realizing at last that no man could reach the goal of enlightenment by striving after it, he decided to sit down and wait.

Let my skin wither, my hands grow numb, my bones dissolve; until I have attained understanding I will not rise from here.

He took up his position on a throne of grass which he had made for himself, folded his legs into the lotus posture and entered into meditation. As he sat, Mara, the spirit of temptation, tried all the tricks he knew to make him give up his quest.

In the first watch of the night Gautama's mind went back over his former lives, and he felt pity for all the people in the world who were still tied to the endless cycle of birth and death.

In the second watch of the night he acquired the 'heavenly eye' of insight, and was able to see the world as it really was. He found 'nothing substantial in the world of becoming, just as no core of heartwood is found in a plantain tree when its layers are peeled off one by one'.

In the third watch of the night he meditated on the real nature of the world. He saw how all things begin in ignorance and lead on to old age and death.

In the fourth watch, 'when dawn broke and all the ghosts that move, and those that move not went to rest', Siddhartha Gautama reached the state of all-knowledge, and so became the Buddha—The Enlightened One. In joy he cried out,

> Many a house of life
> Hath held me—seeking ever him who wrought
> These prisons of the senses, sorrow fraught;
> Sore was my ceaseless strife!
> But now,
> Thou builder of this dwelling—thou!
> I know thee! Never shalt thou build again
> These walls of pain.

For seven days he sat under the tree, unaware of his body, his eyes never closing. He still had one decision to make. He had reached the end of the path. He could therefore leave the body for which he had no longer any further use, or he could keep it so that he could go back into the world and share what he had discovered. He wondered whether he would achieve anything by returning; it could be that he would even make things worse for his fellow beings by taking his knowledge to them. In the end, however, he knew that he could not keep his discovery to himself, so he rose and walked back the way he had come.

THE TEACHING OF THE BUDDHA

The Buddha was 35 years old when he walked away from the place of enlightenment, and he continued to teach the

Government of India Tourist Office

The Buddha's first sermon at Deer Park to his five comrades

way until he reached extreme old age. His first pupils were
the five ascetics who had rejected him when he had given
up the austere life. When they saw him coming towards
them they were prepared to mock the man who had
turned back towards the soft life. Then they noticed
something new and strangely commanding about his
manner which made them listen to what he had to say.

First he drew a wheel on the ground to illustrate the
cycle of existence, then he laid out the heart of his
message. Enlightenment was not to be found either in
following the pleasures of the worldly life, on the one
hand, or in excessive self discipline, on the other. The path
to be followed lay along the *middle way* between the two
extremes of indulgence and asceticism. He taught them the
four noble truths of existence.

a) All life consists of suffering.
b) Suffering is caused by desire.
c) The cure of suffering is the elimination of desire.
d) Desire can be eliminated by following the Noble
Eightfold Path.

The Buddha was not the first to teach that all life consists of suffering. An old Indian story described man's condition in very vivid terms. He is like a traveller wandering, lost and alone in a jungle full of wild beasts, who falls into a pit, which has been covered over with creepers. At the bottom of the pit is a serpent, waiting to eat him, but, as he falls the creepers grasp his leg and he is left hanging, head downwards. For a time the wretched man gets some pleasure catching drops of honey from a comb, which is at the edge of the pit, but, even as he eats, he can see that mice are gnawing at the roots of the tree on which the creepers are growing. In time the tree will fall, and he will be pitched headlong into the pit, where he will be devoured by the snake. This might appear a somewhat pessimistic answer to the question 'Who am I?' We would not be surprised if it prompts the answer, 'Stop the world, I want to get off!'

Despite its stress on the fact that all is suffering, the Buddha's teaching is not pessimistic because he leads his disciples further towards the goal of enlightenment. Every individual is strapped to the wheel of birth and death by the strength of his own desires. The Hindus said that man must liberate himself; Buddhists prefer to use the term *enlightenment* to describe that moment when an individual at last breaks free from the wheel. The goal of all existence is the state of *nirvana*. This is taken from an old Aryan word which means 'to blow'. This final state of bliss comes when all desires have vanished and the Self is blown out.

Buddhism draws many ideas from its mother religion of Hinduism. The Enlightened One broke sharply with the past, however, when he pointed to the way in which his disciples should search for enlightenment.

He rejected the sacrifices of popular devotion as well as the caste structure of society and all the duties that went with it. Hindu seekers after liberation had to go to gurus and follow the path of yoga step by step. The Buddha threw his followers back on their own resources. He could show them the way, but they had to follow it for themselves. For their guidance he offered his *noble eight-*

fold path.

1. The first step lies in *right understanding*. Before any seeker can start the journey to enlightenment, he must understand the true nature of existence, and recognize that all is suffering.

2. Secondly he must have *right motives*—that is, he must know where he wants to go. This means that he must have compassion to all men and genuinely wish to break free from desire.

3. The Seeker demonstrates his control over himself and concern for other people by *right speech*. He should be kind and considerate to others and preserve silence when he has nothing significant to say.

4. The Buddha insisted that his followers should live out their religion in their lives. *Right action* was therefore essential to any progress along the path. We will look closer at the moral guidance which he laid down for his disciples (pages 53-4).

5. No one would be able to make progress whose daily occupation led him to perform acts which conflicted with the ultimate objectives of his life. A *right means of livelihood* was therefore essential.

6. Once the seeker had set his path, he had to exert a *right effort* in working towards his goal. Both over-anxiety and striving on the one hand, and sloth and idleness on the other had to be avoided.

7. By the proper ordering of his life the seeker would be able to achieve *right mind control*. This would be realized by mental discipline and the practise of meditation.

8. This will lead to the last step in the Eightfold Path, the final goal of the Buddhist life, which is *right serenity*.

This advice was intended as a signpost, not as a set of detailed instructions. The Buddha himself described his teaching as a raft, which was useful enough to get somebody from one bank of a river to another, but then had to be abandoned.

If one has crossed with the help of a raft a great stretch of water, on this side full of doubts and fears, on the further side safe and free from fears, one would not take it on one's shoulder and carry it with one. But though it was of great use to him, he would leave it behind, having finished with it. Thus, brethren, understanding the figure of the raft, we must leave rightous ways behind, not to speak of unrighteous ways.

He never demanded obedience from his followers, but asked rather that they should take decisions for themselves. He never said 'You must not', but only 'Would it not be better if you refrained from—?'

It was hard for the seeker after enlightenment to understand that all life consists of suffering and to learn to accept that suffering. On one occasion a mother brought her dead child and asked the Buddha to perform a miracle and bring it back to life. The Master told her to go and collect a mustard seed from a household which has never known death and bring it back to him. In time she returned without the seed. She had found no such household. The Buddha did not perform any miracle, but the mother learnt to accept her loss. Her grief was matched by the grief of countless others.

The whole structure of right and wrong was built upon the *compassion* which arises out of a sense of the unity of all mankind, bound together in suffering. On one occasion the master found a monk dying, lonely and neglected. As he settled down to ease the man's last hours he advised his followers, 'He who would wait on me, let him wait on the sick.'

The same sense of compassion was to be extended to other living creatures. The Buddhist scriptures lay great stress on reverence for all life.

As I am, so are these. As these are, so am I. Thus identifying himself with others the wise man neither kills nor causes to be killed.
Whoso strives only for his own happiness, and in so doing hurts or kills living creatures which also seek for happiness, he shall find no happiness after death.

Having laid down the principle, however, the Master left his followers free to interpret it for themselves. Some Buddhists carry the reverence for life to great lengths, walking with care and brushing seats before they sit down for fear of crushing small insects; others do not go to such extremes. Some are vegetarians; others eat meat. Nearly all have a gentleness which seems strange to the more violent people of Europe and America.

Theft was ruled out for the Buddhist, and the term included many actions which are considered legal in the Western world. The seeker after enlightenment had to cut himself free from all those earthly desires which kept him in the cycle of rebirth. It was obvious, therefore, that he should not try to get hold of things that were not rightly his.

Sexual desire in the same way had to be overcome. The Buddha himself, as we have seen, had experienced the normal human pleasures before he left his father's home, and did not suggest that sex was in itself wrong or unclean. He did, however, recommend the seeker after enlightenment to master those emotions of desire—for food and possessions as well as sexual pleasure—which kept him on the wheel. He taught his male followers to treat the female sex with some caution. When the master lay on his death bed, his disciple Ananda asked for guidance.

'How are we to conduct ourselves, Lord, with regard to women?"
"Do not see them, Ananda."
"But if we should see them, what are we to do?"
"Abstain from speech."
"But if they speak to us, Lord, what are we to do?"
"Keep wide awake, Ananda."

It is fair to say, however, that he did allow women to join his order (see page 62), and so opened the way of enlightenment to them as well.

The Buddhist also had to learn to respect the truth. This did not merely mean that he should not tell specific lies, but also that he should refrain from exaggerating, and discipline himself to think truthfully.

The last of the moral guidelines is that the Buddhist should not allow his mind to become clouded by drink or drugs. In our own day many who claim to admire the teaching of the Master seem to think that the goal of enlightenment can be reached with the help of hallucinatory drugs. The Buddha himself strongly repudiated the idea. According to his teaching true enlightenment can only be achieved by a clear, controlled mind.

The Buddha's message was essentially practical. He was not concerned to answer deep questions about life and death, but to guide people on a path which would take them away from suffering. He would not be drawn into speculating about the nature of God, or what happened to people after death. Arguing about such matters only served to distract people's minds from the real issues confronting them. If a man was shot by a poisoned arrow, he said, he would not be likely to waste his time asking questions about the individual who fired the shaft—whether he was married or not, whether he was tall or short, whether he was fair or dark. His one concern would be to get the arrow out of his body.

No unenlightened man could see the whole truth of life and death. One day some of the Buddha's followers came and told him that a number of holy men were creating a disturbance, arguing about the nature of existence. To explain the futility of this he told a story. Once upon a time, he said, a ruler called together all the blind men in his city and stood them round an elephant. He then told them to describe the animal. One of the blind men grasped the creature's head and declared that the elephant was a large pot. Another found an ear, and said that he had got hold of a winnowing fan. A third discovered the tusk and announced that the object was a ploughshare. Yet another felt the tuft at the end of the creature's tail, and insisted that the elephant was a broom. The point he was making is that the truth can look different from different angles, and no one can see more than a part of it at any time. Little therefore is gained by speculation and argument.

Buddhism therefore neither affirms nor denies the existence of God. Every man and woman must find the truth where they will, and, in general Buddhists have been very tolerant in allowing others to disagree with their own point of view. One thing is true of the whole Indian tradition—be it Hindu or Buddhist. God—or the Supreme Essence—or Brahman or whatever it is called, is never looked upon as something separate from man; I (subject), God (object)—a being living somewhere 'out there'. A man cannot seek God by thinking about him, but only by living in the world, and by being aware of the things around him. On one occasion the disciples gathered round to hear the Enlightened One preach. All he did was to pick a flower and hold it up silently in front of them. Many were puzzled at what such a lesson could mean, but it is recorded that one disciple just smiled and understood the things which go beyond words.

In the 6th Century B.C., when the Buddha taught, Hindus spent a great deal of time in profitless controversy about the nature of the Self—that indestructable and divine part of each creature. They asked what it was like and where it was to be found. Some went as far as to say that it was something hard, the size of a thumb, located within the heart. The holy men who quarrelled about such issues were doing nothing to help simple people find an answer to their question, "Who am I?"

The Buddha cut through all the argument about the relationship of the individual to the universe with the remarkable statement, 'There is no Self'. It is certainly alarming for anyone asking the question, 'Who am I?' to be met with the answer, 'There's no such person!' Of course, the Buddha did not deny that in a certain sense we do exist as individuals. On one occasion he said,

I declare to you that within the body, although it is mortal and only six feet long, you can find the world, and the path that leads to all goals.

But the Buddha held a view of matter which is strikingly similar to that now accepted by modern scientists. All things, he said, are subject to change. The world around us may look very solid, but in reality it is as impermanent as a cobweb at dawn, sparkling with a thousand drops of dew. If this is true of all the objects which surround us, it is no less true of ourselves. Our bodies progress through the processes of childhood, maturity and old age. Our minds flit from one object to another like a monkey swinging its way through a forest grasping first one branch and then another.

The thing that we call 'I' is not, therefore, something solid and permanent. Many Hindus would probably have said that even an inanimate object like a chariot had a 'self', which was in some way part of the great, divine Self. But the Buddha said that a chariot is just a thing of parts—wheels, axles, shafts. In just the same way man is also a thing of parts. He responds to the world through his senses and emotions. We can define the parts as we will—the Buddha separated them into *five heaps*; the body, the feelings, the perceptions, the impulses and emotions, the acts of consciousness. All of these— themselves in a constant state of change—are bundled together into a single human being. But, when we look beyond the five heaps to find the Self, we discover only the emptiness of the Void, a mirror which reflects the world but has no being of its own.

It is very hard for Westerners to understand this central idea of No-Self because we have all been brought up to believe that the Self is the only real and permanent thing in the whole world. A very small child, it is true, has no sense of his own separate existence. You can ask baby John 'Where's Mummy?', 'Where's Daddy?', 'Where's sister Jane?' and he will proudly point to each. But when you ask him, 'Where's Johnny?' he will look around bewildered. Mothers spend a lot of time and trouble teaching Johnny just where he is. 'You show Mummy where your mouth is' and 'Where's your nose?' After this first geography lesson, little Johnny has to be taught to 'stand up for himself'. By the time that he goes to school he has been thoroughly indoctrinated with the idea that he exists as something completely separate from all other objects. This stress on the individual comes partly from the Western religious tradition; partly from the very aggressive society in which we and our ancestors have been reared. In our society it is indeed necessary to teach Johnny very early that life is a rat race, and he has got to fight to keep his end up.

The path of enlightenment, which the Buddha taught, involves a reversal of this whole process. The moment of nirvana—of blowing out —comes when the Self disappears, when 'I' is no longer the subject of the sentence and 'the world' the object. If we find it hard to understand we need not be surprised. The Buddha did not put the concept of No-Self forward as something to be *understood*, but as something to be *discovered*.

Many centuries after the Buddha's death a monk asked the Chinese master, Hui Neng, who should be looked up to as the Zen Buddhist patriarch (religious leader).

"One who understands Buddhism," replied Hui Neng.
"Is that you?" asked the monk.
"No," replied Hui Neng.
"Why not?"
"Because I do not understand Buddhism."

It was agreed that Hui Neng's reply proved conclusively that he was the patriarch!

THE DEATH OF THE BUDDHA

The Buddha was first and foremost a teacher—arguably the greatest teacher of all time. He presented men with his message, but would never force anyone to believe anything, for every individual had to stand on his own feet. The last words which he spoke as he lay dying, probably in the year 483 B.C. as an old man of 80, rammed home the message of self reliance. 'Decay is inherent in all compound things,' he said. 'Be unto yourselves a refuge. Strive mindfully.' Then, as his followers believe, he entered the highest state of consciousness from which there is no return, which he had delayed for 45 years so that he could share his wisdom. He had not taught everything that he knew, but only such parts of the truth as could be of value to men.

After the Master had died, one of his disciples begged the others not to mourn for him.

If all that is born contains within itself the seeds of dissolution, how is it possible that this body too shall not be dissolved?

He was cremated in Hindu fashion, and seven days later the ashes were divided into ten parts, which were given to the rulers of the land in which he had worked. Shrines were built to house his remains, and these soon became the centre for the kind of religious observance which the Buddha himself had repudiated.

Soon after the Master's death his followers met together to go over his teaching so that they could pass it on faithfully. Thus, although his words were not committed to writing for about four centuries, it is reasonable to assume that the basic core of the teaching was handed down accurately.

Most teachers live undramatic lives, and the Buddha was no exception to this rule. There are many stories of miracles which he performed, but it is probably true to say that Buddhists are less concerned than Christians about whether such details in the narrative of their founder's birth and life are strictly true. The deeper meaning is more important than the literal history. Buddhists artists have, for instance, loved to depict an incident in the Master's life when his cousin tried to kill him by turning a wild elephant loose on the path along which he was walking. The Buddha had been warned of his intention, but refused to change his route. The animal charged down on him, but as it came close it felt the great power of the Master's compassion, so that instead of crushing him, as had been intended, it knelt down in homage as the Buddha walked past. Whether true or not, it is a vivid parable of the force of love which lay at the heart of all the Enlightened One's teaching.

(opposite) *One of the gold plated statues inside the walls of the temple of the Emerald Buddha, Bangkok*

KING ASOKA

The same moral is pointed, this time in reliably historical terms, in the life of the great king, Asoka Maurya, who came to the throne in 270 B.C. He inherited a powerful empire, and, following his caste duty, set about expanding his power further over the Indian sub-continent. The early years of his reign were taken up with bloodshed and conquest. But, at the end of his last great battle, he stood on Dhanli Hill and looked over the dreadful carnage on the field below. At that moment he determined to embrace the Buddha's path of non-violence. He carved his intention on the rock of the hill, and recorded his decrees in other rock carvings which can still be read today.

Asoka dedicated the rest of his reign to the improvement of his people's lot. To this end he had wells dug and reservoirs constructed. He built hospitals for the sick, and even for animals. He persecuted no one for his beliefs, but did everything that he could to spread the teachings of the Buddha, not only within India, but outside as well. Tradition says that Asoka's own son set off on a mission to Ceylon, which remains a stronghold of the religion today. For some time after Asoka's reign Buddhism was the dominant religion in the Indian sub-continent, but it was later to be overcome by revivals of popular Hinduism. The teaching had in the meantime spread outwards to other parts of Asia where, except in Communist China it still flourishes.

THE TWO SCHOOLS

At about the time of Asoka a division was beginning to open out between the two major schools of Buddhism, the *Theravada* (southern school) and the *Mahayana* (northern school). Although they disagree sharply on their interpretation of the Buddha's teaching, they have both been true to its spirit in that they have avoided persecuting each other, as rival groups in other religions have all too often done.

Theravada Buddhism

The word Theravada means 'doctrine of the elders', and it is the proud boast of southern Buddhists that they preserve the pure teaching of the Buddha. Certainly their sacred text, the Pali Canon, was written down considerably earlier than any Mahayana books.

Theravada Buddhists lay the main emphasis on the search of the individual for enlightenment. They have little to say about God, except to deny his existence altogether. Large portions of the populations of Ceylon and Burma are therefore living repudiations of the Western assumption that it is impossible to be an atheist and religious at one and the same time, for they are, indeed, among the most religious people on earth.

'Be a refuge unto yourselves. Strive mindfully', advised the Buddha; his Theravada followers take this advice very literally. The disciplines of meditation have been practised for centuries and perfected to a fine art. Merchants, housewives and all kinds of working people take time out of their busy lives to follow the path of enlightment at one of the many meditation centres scattered around the country. There they spend long hours seeking to discover the truth of No-Self. In the course of their hours of meditation they go through powerful experiences— sometimes of intense pain, sometimes of overwhelming joy. Followers of all religions have told of similar experiences.

These cannot be described properly in words, but perhaps some flavour may be gained by following the experience of one Australian woman who spent some weeks at a meditation centre in Burma. Her practice was based on the two words 'phyit-pyet'. These mean 'in-out'—the in-out of breathing, of creation and destruction of the endless cycle of the universe. She describes the emotions which she experienced when she started to practice meditation.

There were violent stabs of pain like red-hot needles and always, it seemed, on the tenderest parts of the anatomy. They got worse and worse. They recalled Mara's assaults on the Buddha the night he attained enlightenment. I did not dare to move lest they should stop before they departed naturally, and repeated almost aloud and almost violently 'phyit-pyet', taking deep breaths to make the pain bearable. A stimulant to greater effort was how U Thein had explained them. Right, more effort there should be, and the 'phyit-pyet' flowed fast and furious; one would hardly have called it successful meditation, but it was certainly vigorous. The javelin thrusts were interspersed with worms tickling almost unbearably, but the pain was worse than the tickling. However, at last both the stabs and the worms got fewer and finally died away, and I turned to contemplate with great equanimity the 'phyit-pyet' on the heart. As I looked mentally the heart turned into a whirling top, faster, faster, faster! It seemed to be drawing the rest of the body into it. I looked on fascinated. Then all of a sudden, without any warning, it disintegrated, leaving only a sea of atoms and a rather exhausted body floating at peace upon that sea. I do no know how long I lay, too enthralled to move. But the drama gradually ended and concentration became normal again.

This is the beginning of the path. Beyond these turbulent emotions lies the peace of utter stillness, reached by those who persist with patience.

Although such experiences can be achieved by ordinary people, leading normal lives, it has been generally assumed by Theravada Buddhists that final enlightenment is attainable only by those who bind themselves completely to the religious life by becoming members of the *sangha* (order of monks).

Travellers to the East soon become aware of the yellow robed monks who wander with their begging bowls round the streets of the towns in all Theravada Buddhist countries. The Master himself organized his followers into the sangha, and, with some hesitation, he admitted women as well as men. When someone wishes to join the order he makes the ancient threefold statement,

I take refuge in the Buddha.
I take refuge in the dharma (teaching).
I take refuge in the sangha.

(opposite) *A young Burmese boy who has become a priest, with his begging bowl*

He then has his head shaved, takes certain vows, puts on his yellow robe and is given a begging bowl. Unlike a Christian monk, a Buddhist monk is not tied by his vows for life. He can leave the order any time he wishes. As long as he remains in the community, however, he is expected to abide by its rules.

Monks are greatly respected in Theravada countries as long as they live up to the strict code laid down for them. Their lives are governed by 227 rules. They must eat temperately, and not at all after noon; they are not allowed to watch dancing, listen to singing or go to plays; they may not wear any kind of personal adornment, they must sleep on hard beds and can never handle money. The only possessions a monk needs are his robe, his begging bowl and a filter to strain any living creatures out of the water which he drinks. Within the sangha the seeker after enlightenment can work out his own salvation with real diligence.

Mahayana Buddhism

The difference between the Theravada and the Mahayana branches of Buddhism is well illustrated in a little story. A pious woman allowed a monk to build himself a shelter at the bottom of her garden, where he could meditate. For seven years he sat there, seeking enlightenment. At the end of that time the woman's daughter decided to see whether she could use her sex appeal to tempt him away from his contemplation. She tried every way that she could to make him take an interest in her but, however hard she tried, the monk just sat, paying no attention to her whatsoever. When the woman who owned the house heard of the incident, she threw the monk out of her garden. "I didn't expect you to fall for my daughter's tricks," she said, "but you might at least have taken some interest in the girl."

The monk's attitude was that of a Theravada Buddhist. The one thing that mattered was his personal enlightenment; nothing was to be allowed to get in its way. The mother's attitude was that of a Mahayana Buddhist; human compassion was to her the supreme duty of a holy man. In Mahayana Buddhism the holy man's resolution is not, 'May I become a Buddha and attain enlightenment,' but 'May I become a Buddha in order to help every creature who may come to me.'

Theravada is a religion for monks; Mahayana is a religion for laymen. The former allows no concessions to human weakness; the latter is all-embracing and much more easy-going. In Theravada men and women have to live off their own resources. In Mahayana they are given the help of innumerable saints, or *Bodhisatvas*:

Mahayana Buddhists lay great stress on the fact that the Buddha rejected the idea of keeping his enlightenment to himself, but decided instead to share it with all other creatures. Not content with the one historical Buddha, they people the universe with Buddhas. Like Hindus, Buddhists believe that the world is immensely old. Followers of the Mahayana also accept that there are innumerable other inhabited worlds. Far back in time and away out in space are men who have chosen to follow the path of enlightenment, not for their own sake, but so that they can help others.

In Mahayana language, a man who has chosen to postpone his own entry into nirvana for the sake of others is known as a Bodhisattva. When he sets out on the upward path he makes a pledge;

I wish to be bread for the hungry, drink for those who are thirsty. I give myself, all that I am and shall be in my future existences, to all creatures.

Ordinary folk, whose energies are taken up by the hum-drum concerns of daily life can turn to the Bodhisatt-vas for help on the path to enlightenment.

Theravada Buddhists point out that this goes against the Buddha's instruction to all his followers to work out their own salvation. Mahayana Buddhists reply that, while keeping to the letter of the Master's teaching, the southern school miss its spirit because they pay too little attention to the overwhelming demands of human compassion.

While the Theravada is virtually an atheist religion,

Mahayana Buddhists generally feel the need for some saint or deity to whom they can direct their worship. The northern school has been much more open in absorbing the gods of the lands into which their faith spread. The opposite extreme from the severe 'doctrine of the elders' may be found in the astonishing mixture of primitive religion, elaborate ritual and the profoundest Buddhist piety, which flourished in Tibet, until that mountainous country was overrun by Chinese Communists in 1959. A modern Tibetan monk has summed up the way of Mahayana. It is not, he writes,

a way of running away from the world but of overcoming it through growing knowledge, through active love towards one's fellow beings, through inner participation in the joys and sufferings of others, and through equanimity with regard to one's own weal and woe.

Mahayana Buddhism varies greatly from one area to another. The most famous branch of it has developed a distinctive approach which today arouses great interest in many parts of the world. This school, known as Zen, started in China and today has its home in Japan.

Zen Buddhism
We have said that Mahayana Buddhism was inclined to absorb rather than destroy other religions that lay across the path of its expansion. Zen is the product of a union between the Indian teaching of the Buddha and the Chinese way of Taoism.
a) Zen is Buddhist in that it shares with all other schools the fundamental assumptions of the Four Noble Truths (page 49). The follower of Zen seeks the enlightenment of nirvana.
b) Its distinctive flavour, however, is borrowed from the Taoist insistence that life must be wholly natural. Zen Buddhists therefore stress that enlightenment comes by seeing the world as it really is, not by drawing away from it.

We have seen that the Buddha disapproved of abstract questioning which turned attention from the real issues of life. Many later Buddhists, however, spent their time in just such profitless arguments. The Zen masters have had an almost alarming way of cutting through such speculation. One of them went up to a monk who was solemnly practising meditation.

"Your reverence," asked the master, "what is the objective of sitting in meditation?"

"The objective," replied the monk, "is to become a Buddha."

The Zen master immediately picked up a tile from the floor and began to polish it furiously.

"What are you doing, master?" asked the monk.

"I am polishing it for a mirror."

"How could polishing a tile make a mirror?"

"How could sitting in meditation make a Buddha?" replied the master.

It is as hopeless for men to try to solve the riddles of the universe as it is for a mosquito to try to bite an iron bar. All that they can do is to grasp the simple moment as it passes by and try to understand its meaning. The deep realities of life lie in the everyday things.

We eat, execrate, sleep, and get up;
This is our world.
All we have to do after that—
Is to die.

Zen stories are full of humour and seeming illogicality. A few examples will give a taste of the completely unique flavour of the Zen way of thinking.

One day Ma-tsu and Po-chang were out walking when some wild geese flew past.

"What are they?" asked Ma-tsu.

"They're wild geese," replied Po-chang.

"What are they doing?"

"They've already flown away."

At this Ma-tsu grabbed his companion's nose and twisted it until he cried out in pain. "How could they ever have flown away?" he shouted.

The point of the story is that, if man is at one with all

creatures, it is impossible for the geese to fly *away* from him; they must always be coming *towards* him.

"What is the Buddha?" the disciple asked the master T'ung-Shan.

His eye landed on the first concrete object that he saw. "Three pounds of flax," he replied.

The moment of awakening does not come from a withdrawal from the world of concrete objects, like geese and flax, but from participation in them. After days of meditation, when he has been 'sitting quietly doing nothing', the seeker after enlightenment may need some sharp shock—a kick, a blow, a twist of the nose—to make him aware once again of the reality of his own body.

"What is the meaning of Bodhidharma (the founder of Zen) coming from the West?" asked a pupil.

The master made him kneel on the ground and make a deep salaam, and when his bottom was upturned, he kicked it fiercely. It was said that in that moment the pupil gained enlightenment, and afterwards he never stopped laughing.

The greatest virtue in the Zen life is to be natural. One story tells of how a monk could not make up his mind what would be the best position in which to die. Some holy men had chosen to sit in the position of meditation; others followed the example of the Buddha and died lyingon one side. This monk decided that he would try a completely new posture and die standing on his head. He therefore took up this position and duly expired. When the people arrived they were amazed at seeing a dead body upside down and were scared to touch it. Finally the dead man's sister, who was a Zen nun, arrived on the scene.

"When you were alive," she declared, "you took no notice of laws and customs, and even now that you're dead you are making a perfect nuisance of yourself." She then gave the body a good poke so that it toppled over to the ground, and the people took it off to the cremation ground.

Although Zen had its origin in China it flourished in Japan where it has had an immense influence on the whole civilization.

a) Judo is based on the principles of Zen, for it is the 'gentle art' in which the body is allowed to do the work through its own momentum and all striving and tension is eliminated.

b) The famous Japanese tea ceremony, with its elegance and its ritual is essentially a Zen religious rite. It is said that 'the taste of Zen and the taste of tea are one'.

c) Japanese art, and particularly coloured brushwork paintings, draw heavily on Zen. Man has tended to dominate the canvases of western artists, but in Japanese painting he appears as a tiny figure stumping his lonely but undefeated way across broad blank spaces of emptiness, against the overwhelming background of nature.

In contrast to the silence and peace of a Theravada place of meditation, a Zen monastery tends to be a somewhat noisy and vigorous establishment. In monasteries of other Buddhist schools, laymen are employed to do all the dirty work. Relieved of the chores of life, the monks are able to devote their lives to meditation. Zen monasteries, on the other hand, are run on the principle 'No work; then no food!' The monks have to do their own gardening, washing, cooking and cleaning. These tasks are not looked upon as unwelcome chores which break the peace of meditation. Zen meditation involves hard work. Enlightenment is not achieved by running away from everyday things, but by living in the world as it really is. At times teachers yell and shout at their first year pupils. Like the Zen masters of old they seek to give their pupils a sudden awareness of the world in which they live. It is a world of common things, like geese and flax. The human body, set in this world, feels happiness, sadness, pain and pleasure. The Zen teachers seek to bring their pupils to the moment of breakthrough through an awareness of themselves. Zen training was used in the education of the warrior *samurai* class of old Japan, and Zen training gave the Japanese pilots of World War Two the self-discipline to plunge to their deaths on American and British warships.

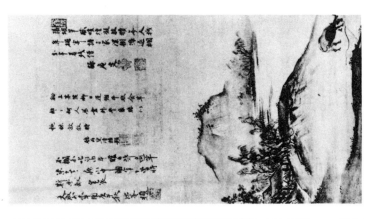

*Landscape by Ma Yuan, showing Zen influence in the utter insignifi-
cance of Man against the background of Nature*

BUDDHISM IN THE WEST

All over the Western world in recent years there has been a growing interest in Buddhist philosophy. In an age of doubt it has the advantage of not putting forward any set pattern of beliefs which the seeker has to accept. Interest is particularly strong in the United States. The island of Hawaii, now a state of the Union, is Buddhist by tradition. More recently the hippies of the West Coast have borrowed much from the teachings of the Master.

Zen has been having a particular vogue in Europe and America. A word of caution has, however, to be given. The Zen concept of being natural and the pop philosophy of 'doing your own thing' are very far from being identical. All the Zen masters assumed that they were teaching their pupils to be natural within the framework of an ordered society. The rules of behaviour both in Confucian China and in Shinto Japan were very strict indeed, and Zen Buddhists were not encouraged, or allowed to flout them. The doctrine of 'doing your own thing' in the West, in contrast, is generally put forward by those who wish to defy the rules of society. Zen teachers themselves insist that, divorced from the guidelines of a settled social structure, their own methods can become highly dangerous.

Nonetheless, the Western world has clearly a great deal to learn from the wisdom of the East, both Hindu and Buddhist. The path of meditation offers a way out of the endless striving and competition which seems inbuilt into modern city life. Even in a technological age man can do well to heed the sermon of the flower, held up in silence by the Buddha.

5
Chosen by God
JUDAISM

That part of the Middle East which is known as the fertile crescent has been described as the cradle of civilization. It was in this area that men first gathered into the larger communities which we call cities, and developed the skills of government and writing.

The great civilizations of ancient times—Sumeria, Egypt, Assyria, Babylon, Persia—rose and fell in the land watered by the three rivers, Tigris, Euphrates and Nile and by the rain blown off the Mediterranean Sea. Here men lived settled lives, cultivating their crops and using the surplus of their wealth to carry on trade. Beyond this green crescent the land produced only sparse vegetation which could not support settled communities. People therefore had to live as *nomads*, wandering with their sheep and cattle in search of good grazing.

The term *Semites* is used to describe a group of tribes which lived a nomadic life around the edges of this settled world. By tradition they were descended from Shem, the son of Noah. They were never a unified nation. In course of time one group abandoned their nomadic existence and established themselves as farmers in the fertile crescent. These people, who called themselves the children of Israel, claimed descent from the common ancestor Jacob, who was Abraham's grandson. The Semites have given the world no less than three of its great religions. From the Israelites came Judaism, and its daughter religion, Christianity. From the tribes that remained in the desert country came Islam.

THE SEMITIC WORLD VIEW

We have seen (page 22) that Indian people had certain assumptions about the world, which formed the basis of all Hindu and Buddhist thinking. In the same way the Semitic people had assumptions which underlie all their three religions.

Perhaps the fundamental difference between Eastern and Western ideas about the universe is that those who take their lead from the Indians see time as moving in endless circles, while those who follow the Semites see it as progressing in a straight line. Jews, Christians and Moslems have traditionally thought of time as having a beginning and an end—like a piece of string. At one end is the Creation. At the other end will be the last days when the time process as we know it will reach its end and men will come face to face with a divine judge.

This is not, however, the whole perspective of the Semitic religions. Beyond the day of judgement there opens up a whole new dimension of everlasting life. A man or woman has only one existence on earth in which to prepare for eternity.

The Creator God
The people of the fertile crescent worshipped a wide variety of gods, which were expected to preserve the fertility of the fields and protect the people from natural disasters. Some of the tribes of the area practised human sacrifice on a large scale. In the city of Ur of the Chaldes, for instance, a dead king was buried with hundreds of servants. The ritual killing of new born children also appears to have been common.

The Book of Genesis tells the story of how Abraham turned his back on this idol worship and chose to be a monotheist. To be free to worship in his own way he left Ur with his family and set off to be a nomad in the desert. In return for this act of renunciation, God promised that he would be the father of a great nation.

will make you into a great nation, I will bless you and make your name so great that it shall be used in blessings.

Abraham has been known as the first Hebrew, and both the Jews and the Moslems (see page 141) look on him as the founder of their religion.

The story of Abraham, which lies deep in prehistory, was handed down by word of mouth for many generations, and it is impossible to tell how far it is historically accurate. It is, however, certainly true to say that one branch of the Semitic people began to worship just one God. It appears that in the early days the Israelites did not deny the existence of other gods. They just assumed that their God was the most powerful, and so could be trusted to defeat all his rivals.

Many of the gods of the ancient world were little more than rather large size versions of human beings or animals. The Hebrews, however, saw their protector as lying far beyond the sphere of mere human understanding. If he could be likened to anything it was fire. When Moses, the greatest leader and prophet of Israel, saw a bush that was burning but was not consumed, he knew that he was in the presence of God. His first reaction was despair. He was a sinner from a sinful people; the sight of the glory of God must surely destroy him. But God had a task for him to do. He was to lead the Israelites out of their bondage in Egypt. Moses was bold enough to ask God his name.

Then Moses said to God, 'If I go to the Israelites and tell them that the God of their forefathers has sent me to them, and they ask me his name, what shall I say?' God answered, 'I AM; that is who I am.'

In one sense God had not answered Moses' question. 'I am' is something of a riddle. It was almost as if he was telling Moses to mind his own business. But 'I am' means also that God is the eternal and absolute being. The Jews' name for God was Yahweh (or, as the Bible spells it, Jehovah), but this name was so holy that they wrote it as YHWH, and spoke it as 'adonai' (= 'Lord').

Once Jews understood God in these terms, they could not conceive of other gods existing alongside him. He was no longer to be thought of as the protector of one particular tribe, but as the creator of the whole world.

In the beginning of creation, when God made heaven and earth.

Yahweh stood alone; all other gods were impostors.

The Israelites saw God as being utterly *holy*. The original meaning of the word 'holy' is 'separate'. The gods of other tribes were just a part of the world—things of wood and stone. Yahveh was *wholly other*. It was therefore impossible to represent him by any sort of idol or image. The Jews would certainly not accept the Hindu view that God and his creation are one and the same thing. God loves his creatures and controls their destinies, but he always remains separate from them.

The word 'holy' also came to mean 'perfect'. In many of the fables of primitive religions we find the gods performing actions that are immoral by any standards. They can be cruel, lustful and vindictive. This is impossible for Yahveh. God is not only eternal in that he stands above time; he is also eternal in that he provides absolute standards of good and evil by which men can order their lives.

It is possible for Hindus and Buddhists to be religious without believing in any God. To Jews such an idea would seem absurd. Week after week they repeat the words from the Bible, which are known as the Shema. 'Hear Oh Israel, the Lord our God, the Lord is one.' That is the cornerstone of their faith.

The Nature of Man

When we contrast the Semitic view of man with that held by Indians it is worth remembering the different sort of environment in which the two people lived. The men who shaped Indian thought grew up in a river valley where nature is rich and fertile. Human beings lived out their lives surrounded by the trees of the forest which give shelter to all kinds of creatures. The Semites, on the other hand, came from the empty regions where even grass is scarce so that men and animals have to struggle for a living in a hostile land. It is not, perhaps, surprising that the former saw themselves as being a *part of* nature, while the latter tended rather to see themselves as being *set over against* other creatures. Unlike the Indians, the Semites did not believe in the cycle of rebirth. No Jew, Moslem or Christian would accept the idea that he might reappear on earth as a dog, a fish or a lizard.

In the Genesis creation myth man is brought into existence on the last day—a creature set apart, fashioned in the image of God.

Then God said, 'Let us make man in our image and likeness to rule the fish in the sea, the birds of heaven, the cattle, all wild animals on earth, and all reptiles that crawl upon the earth.' So God created man in his own image; in the image of God he created him; male and female he created them. God blessed them and said to them, 'Be fruitful and increase, fill the earth and subdue it, rule over the fish in the sea, the birds of heaven, and every living thing that moves upon the earth.' God also said, 'I give you all plants that bear seed everywhere on earth, and every tree bearing fruit yields seed: they shall be yours for food. All green plants I give for food to the wild animals, to all the birds of heaven, and to all reptiles on earth, every living creature.'

Jews have laid emphasis on the fact that man should be considerate towards the lower creatures. The Bible gives specific instructions as to how unnecessary suffering should be avoided. The ox that treads the corn must not be muzzled; slaughtering must be carried out in a humane manner. Even the animals must be given rest on the Sabbath. But consideration is that of a master for his servants. It is unlikely that the Bible writers would have understood what the Indian sage meant when he declared, 'I am food!'

In Semitic thought each man and woman has just one life to live. The Buddha could afford to present his teaching in a 'take it or leave it' manner. If an individual decided not to seek the path of enlightenment in his current existence it did not matter too much. He would have ample opportunity in future lives. The three Semitic religions, on the other hand, could allow man just a single lifetime in which to accept the truth. Thus, while the Buddha could base his teaching on the relaxed principle of 'it would be a good thing if you did or refrained from doing such and such a thing,' Jewish, Christian and Mohammedan teachers all put forward the imperative, *'you must'* — *'you must not'.* A new sense of urgency therefore enters into religion which is unknown in the East. The responsibility is on man; he must choose between good and evil, between life and death.

The Holy People

Originally, as we have seen, the Israelites looked on Yahweh as their own special protector against other gods. Even after they came to see him as the one God whose power extended over all the world, they continued to believe that they were in a special sense *his people.* The Bible writers certainly do not claim that this relationship was based on the fact that the Jews were more deserving than any other people. They are indeed continually criticised as being a particularly 'stubborn' and 'stiff-necked' race, altogether unworthy of receiving God's favour.

The Children of Israel were picked out from all other races so that they could carry out a task laid on them by God. They were to serve as his witnesses in a world that did not acknowledge him. They therefore had to reflect his nature by their behaviour. *As God is holy, so you must be holy. As God is righteous, so you must be righteous.* To be chosen by God gave no grounds for arrogance, but rather imposed a responsibility which could make any man afraid.

We have seen that, when the Aryans entered India, they allowed their beliefs to become merged with those of the people who were there before them. If the Israelites were to carry out the task for which they had been chosen, they would have to remain separate from the Gentiles who lived around them.

The Israelites therefore ordered their lives by a strict code of laws, which they believed to have been delivered to them by God. These laws have been divided into three categories. Central among these were the commandments, of which the Ten Commandments delivered to Moses on Mount Sinai, (see page 83) are the most important. Commandments lay down basic rules of social and moral conduct. Then there are the statutes, which are not based on any particular principle of good or evil but are none the less central to the faith. In this category come all the regulations governing the food which a Jew may eat. Finally there are a variety of customs and ordinances, which have been passed down by word of mouth from one generation to another. Many of the statutes and customs were originally laid down for good practical reasons, but, when circumstances changed, so that the reasons ceased to have any relevance, the people of God continued to observe their ancient traditions.

The Jews have always recognized that these many different rules do not have the same weight. Long before the time of Jesus a rabbi pointed out that the law could be summarized in two commandments. 'Thou shalt love the Lord thy God.' 'Thou shalt love thy neighbour as thyself.' 'The rest,' he said, 'is commentary.' The concept of love therefore lies at the heart of the Jewish, as it lies at the heart of the Christian, religion. The chosen people will be holy as they love their God, and as they demonstrate that love in their dealings one with another.

A HISTORICAL RELIGION

The Old Testament tells the narrative of how God chose the children of Israel and carried them through many crises when they were threatened by their enemies. In the yearly round of worship Jewish people remember and reenact the key events in their early national history. We will try to understand the significance of these historical events through the eyes of a devout Jew as he or she joins in the religious life of the community.

By tradition Jewish worship has centred round three

(opposite) *Rabbi standing before the Ark, open to show the scrolls of the law (Sofer Torah)*

Juliette Radom

focal points; the Temple, the synagogue and the home.

The Temple. During their wanderings in the wilderness the Israelites carried an *ark* with them, which was considered to be the special resting place on earth of that terrifying power which they called the glory of God. Some time after the year 1000 B.C. King Solomon built a temple in Jerusalem at the centre of which was the holiest of holies, which served as its permanent resting place. There, in the heart of the Temple, God was most truly with his people. No sacrifice could be offered except at the Temple. Solomon's Temple was destroyed by the Babylonians but it was rebuilt after the Israelites were released from captivity. This second Temple was finally destroyed by the Romans shortly after the time of Christ. It was then no longer possible for Jews to make any sacrifices, for they had no Temple in which to make them. At the same time the special order of *priests*, set aside to make the sacrifices to God on behalf of men, disappeared.

The Synagogue. Before the final destruction of the Temple a large number of Jews had settled in distant countries. Many travelled to Jerusalem for the great festivals when they were able to do so, but they clearly needed some centre for worship which was nearer their homes. These Jews of the Dispersion therefore gathered into communities, which became known as synagogues. 10 adult males can establish a synagogue and any one of them may conduct the services. In practice, however, most synagogues have a *rabbi*, or teacher. He is the natural leader of the community, not because his position is especially holy, like the priests of the Temple, but because he knows more of the law than any other member of the synagogue.

The Family. Each Jewish family in itself is a religious unit. Every meal is a religious occasion, and many of the great ceremonies of Judaism are performed within this family circle. Children are brought up to obey the words of the commandment;

Honour your father and your mother, that you may live long in the land which the Lord your God is giving you.

It is noteworthy that rates for juvenile delinquency are always very low in Jewish communities.

A Barmitzvah boy at the age of 13 becomes a man, and sings or reads a special portion from the Torah in the Synagogue.

Juliette Radom

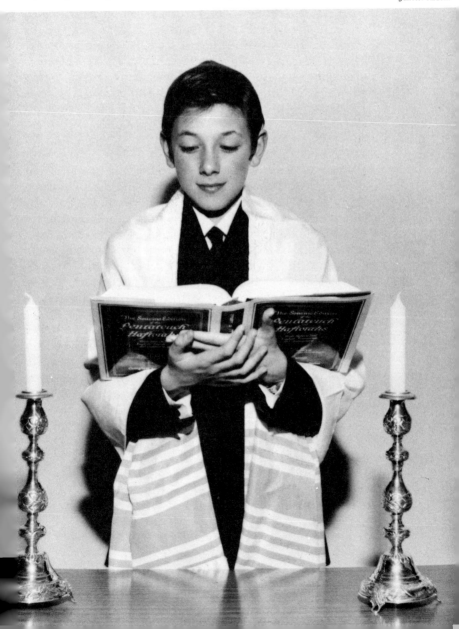

The Jewish Year
There are a number of festivals in which the Jews, either
with joy or sadness, remember the great events of their
history. The three most important are the pilgrim festivals
of Passover, Pentecost, and Tabernacle. Each of these
commemorates a significant event in the crucial forty years
between leaving Egypt and arriving in the Promised Land.
Each is also a harvest festival. Passover celebrates the barley,
Pentecost the wheat and Tabernacles the harvest of the
fruit trees. It is open to question which meaning was the
earlier. Today the seasons of Palestine are remembered in
synagogues all over the world, but the commemorative
significance of the three pilgrim festivals is much the more
important.

The Passover
At Passover time the Jews remember the story of the
deliverance of their people from slavery in Egypt which is
told in the first 15 chapters of the Book of Exodus. The
dramatic events are well known—of how Moses confronted
Pharaoh and demanded that he should let the children of
Israel go; of how plagues were sent onto the Egyptians
until at last the angel of the Lord came over the city and
killed all the firstborn sons of the Egyptians; of how
Pharaoh told the Israelites to leave and then changed his
mind and tried to stop them.

Year by year the Jews act out the story of their
deliverance. The drama centres round the night when the
last plague was sent on Egypt. The Israelites waited inside
their houses, eating a meal in a standing position, ready to
go when the word was given. Moses had instructed them to
take their bread unleavened, that is without any yeast to
make it rise. The lintels of their doors were marked with
the blood of a lamb which they had sacrificed. When the
angel of death came he *passed over* the Israelites houses.
The next morning they took their baggage and animals
and left Egypt. The Bible gave instructions as to how the
Israelites should remember their deliverance.

When you enter the land which the Lord will give you as he promised, you shall observe this rite. Then, when your children ask you, "What is the meaning of this rite?" you shall say, "It is the Lord's Passover, for he passed over the houses of the Israelites in Egypt when he struck the Egyptians but spared our houses."

In this, the best loved of all the festivals, the Jewish family remembers these events. Before Passover time members of the family search through the house to find any food which has any leaven in it, and during the festival days they cook in special pans which have never been used for leavened food. A special dish of bitter herbs is served up, and the children ask, 'Why are we eating this?' 'It reminds us of the bitterness of our captivity in Egypt,' answers their father. Another dish is made up from apples, nuts, cinnamon and wine. 'Why do we eat this?' ask the children. 'It reminds us of the bricks and mortar with which we worked when we were slaves in Egypt,' comes the reply. In the days when sacrifices were made in the Temple at Jerusalem a lamb was offered up by every family. Today there are no sacrifices but the roasted shank bone of a lamb serves as a reminder of that old ceremony.

Passover celebrates the birth of Israel as a nation. It is therefore by tradition a time of happiness.

Pentecost

Pentecost means 'the festival of weeks', for it falls seven weeks after the second day of Passover. This is the time when Jews remember the giving of the law. After leaving Egypt the Israelites lived as nomads in the bleak country of the Arabian peninsula. During this time Moses was told to climb Mount Sinai alone. There he received the tablets of the law on which were inscribed the Ten Commandments.

These commandments are fundamental to the Jewish way of life, but we have seen that a pious Jew was expected to observe many other regulations. Some are taken from the Bible itself; others are derived from later tradition.

a) The *Torah*. The first five books of the Bible are collectively known as the Torah. These regulations have set the pattern of Jewish life. In the east wall of every synagogue there is a special Holy Ark where these most sacred books are kept. The Torah itself is written by hand in a specially prescribed manner on parchment scrolls and is brought out in synagogue services.

b) The *Mishnah*. The collection of the traditional laws, which were not included in the Bible, are also held to be binding on Jews. These writings are treated with scarcely less respect than the Torah itself.

The Jew is taught to look upon the law which regulates his life, not as a restriction to his freedom, but as his privilege and joy. By tradition it is at Pentecost that a child receives his first instruction in the Torah. A drop of honey is placed on a page of the book and he is told to kiss it. The lesson he then learns is supposed to remain with him for the rest of his life; the taste of the Torah is sweet.

Tabernacles
According to the Bible the years of wandering in the wilderness was a period of great physical hardship for the Israelites. At times they were on the edge of starvation, but God then sent them tiny pieces of bread, called manna, and quails to see them through their difficulties. For shelter they had to rely on roughly constructed booths, or tabernacles.

At the feast of Tabernacles Jews build themselves booths in the gardens of their houses. The roof has to be woven loosely enough for the people inside to be able to see the stars at night, and, of course, for the autumn rain to get through. In these booths the family eats its meals, and if it is at all possible, sleeps at night to remember the days when their forefathers lived in conditions of hardship. There are also celebrations at the synagogue. The climax of these comes when the congregation walks around the outside of the building, clasping the scrolls of the law over their hearts.

The New Year
The three pilgrim festivals celebrate particular events in
Israel's national history. At New Year the emphasis is laid
more on the individual. In Christian countries the New
Year is not primarily a religious festival, but provides an
excuse for lighthearted celebration. In contrast, the
Jewish New Year is a solemn—though certainly not a
miserable—occasion. It is the time when each man, woman
and child pauses to remember the sins which he has
committed during the past year.

The New Year is greeted quietly and soberly. Everyone
eats an apple dipped in honey and wishes each other a
sweet and happy New Year. In the synagogue a ram's horn
is blown to mark the beginning of the ten days of
repentance. The blowing of the horn brings many mem-
ories to the worshippers. It reminds them of the ram which
was found in the thicket when Abraham was about to

*The Festival of Tabernacles and Harvest Festival, in memory of the
journey in the wilderness*

Juliette Radom

sacrifice Isaac. It reminds them of the horn that was blown as a warning when the Temple was about to fall. Most of all, it is a call to remind them of their sins. In the words of the prophet Amos, 'If a trumpet sounds the alarm, are not the people scared?' In the afternoon the people go to the bank of a river or to the sea shore and throw crumbs out onto the water to symbolise their sins which will be separated from them. As they do so they quote the words of the prophet Micah, 'and you will cast all your sins into the depth of the sea.'

The days of repentance come to a close with the most solemn day in the Jewish calendar. At the time when the Temple stood in Jerusalem, the High Priest went alone into the holiest of holies, and there sprinkled the blood of a sacrificed animal. This act brought the people back to be *at one* with God. Hence it was called the Day of Atonement (Yom Kippur).

Sacrifices are no longer offered and there can be no priest to stand between the individual and his God. The individual therefore has to find his own repentance for the sins he has committed. Before Yom Kippur, Jews search their hearts so that they may become at one with God and their fellow men. No one can expect his sins to be forgiven unless he approaches Yom Kippur in a proper spirit. He must have put right any wrongs he may have done to his fellow men, and seriously mean to live in accordance with the law. In the words of the Mishnah:

If a man says, "I will sin and repent, and sin again and repent," he will be given no chance to repent. If he says, "I will sin and the Day of Atonement will effect atonement", then the Day of Atonement effects no atonement. For transgressions which are between man and God, the Day of Atonement effects atonement; but for transgressions that are between man and his fellow, the Day of Atonement effects atonement only if he has appeased his fellow.

Israel Government Tourist Office

(opposite) *A shofar, 300 years old, blown by a Yemenite on Mount Zion, near King David's tomb*

THE SABBATH

The three great festivals come round once a year, but every week the Jew has the solemn duty to keep the Sabbath laid down in the commandment.

You have six days to labour and do all your work. But the seventh day is a sabbath of the Lord your God; that day you shall not do any work, your son or your daughter, your slave or your slave-girl, your cattle or the alien within your gates; for in six days the Lord made heaven and earth, the sea, and all that is in them, and on the seventh day he rested. Therefore the Lord blessed the sabbath day and declared it holy.

The idea of a day of rest has much to commend it on practical grounds. A person can work more efficiently if he or she has a regular time to relax and forget the cares of making a living. In the ancient world wealthy people lived a life of ease, while the lower orders worked throughout the hours of daylight for seven days a week. But, when the Israelites were instructed to rest, they were not allowed to make exceptions for their servants, for non-Jews who were living with them, or even for their domestic animals.

The practical virtues of the Sabbath are, however, secondary to its religious significance. God created the earth in six days and rested on the seventh. So man, by resting on the seventh remembers the work of creation.

All mourning and fasting are prohibited on the Sabbath. The people wear their best clothes and eat food of rather better quality than they would normally be able to afford. On the Friday evening the mother of the house lights candles to show that the day of cheer and light has begun. They stand on a table, which symbolizes the altar of the Temple, along with loaves and wine.

There are synagogue services on the Sabbath, but the festival centres on each individual family. The father blesses his children in words used by Jacob over his sons. At the end of the day the last chapter of the Book of Proverbs is recited in honour of the mother.

Who can find a capable wife?
Her worth is far beyond coral.
Her husband's whole trust is in her,
and children are not lacking.
She repays him with good, not evil,
all her life long.
She chooses wool and flax
and toils at her work.
Like a ship laden with merchandise,
she brings home food from far off.
She rises while it is still night
and sets meat before her household.

Work is forbidden on the Sabbath, and the term 'work' is strictly defined. The Torah forbids anyone to light a fire and orthodox Jews have decided that this prohibition extends to turning on a light switch. To the outsider it seems that the Sabbath must be spoilt by the host of such niggling restrictions. Generations of Jews, however, have found it a day of joy and peace. The German writer Heine described how one of his characters spent his Sabbath.

Making Kiddush (blessing over wine) on the Sabbath

Juliette Radom

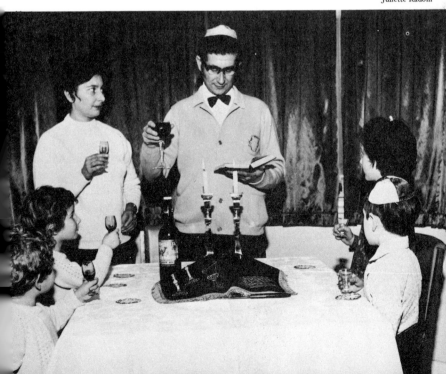

There lives at Hamburg, in a one roomed lodging in the Baker's Broad Walk, a man whose name is Moses Lump. All the week he goes out in the wind and rain, with his pack on his back, to earn his few shillings. But when on Friday evening he comes home, he finds the candlesticks with seven candles lighted, and the table covered with a fair white cloth, and he puts away from him his pack and his cares, and he sits down to table with his squinting wife and his yet more squinting daughter, and eats fish with them, fish which has been dressed in beautiful white garlic sauce, sings therewith the grandest psalms of King David, rejoices with his whole heart over the deliverance of Israel out of Egypt, rejoices too that all the wicked ones who have done the children of Israel hurt, have ended by taking themselves off; that King Pharaoh, Nebuchadnezzer, Hanan, Antiochus, Titus, and all other such people, are well dead, while he, Moses Lump, is yet alive, and eating fish with his wife and daughter; and I tell you, Doctor, the fish is delicate and the man is happy.

THE PROPHETS

As we have seen, rules and regulations are an essential part of the Jewish way of life. At the same time Judaism is not only made up of rules and regulations. From the time of Moses a series of prophets delivered in the most forceful possible manner, the message that it was useless for anyone to go through the motions of being religious if they failed to live up to what they profess.

The word *prophet* is generally used to describe someone who is able to foretell the future. The Israelite prophets did indeed sometimes say what was going to happen, but the future that they foretold was the inevitable result of men's sins in the present. Essentially a prophet was a *forth-teller*, rather than a *fore-teller* that is, he was a man who spoke out fearlessly.

Kings in the ancient world were generally surrounded by courtiers who told them only what they wanted to hear. But the kings of Israel were forced to listen to the words of a succession of independent minded men. While unscrupulous rulers of other nations could make themselves rich at the expense of their wretched subjects, the king of Israel had to respect every man's rights.

A well known story tells how King Ahab wanted a vineyard which belonged to a common man named Naboth. He tried to buy it in the proper way, but Naboth refused to sell. At this point Ahab's wife, Jezebel, who was not a Jew and so did not understand the customs of the people, suggested that he had the power to get anything he wanted. Naboth was therefore taken to court on a false charge, found guilty, and executed. With the legal owner safely out of the way, Ahab took over the vineyard. It was the sort of injustice that happened every day in most countries. But Ahab did not get away with it. He was hounded by the fierce prophet Elijah who pronounced the King's doom.

Later prophets hammered home the same lesson. Amos, the wild shepherd from the hills, for instance, warned of the punishment which would come on those who took advantage of the poor and the helpless.

These are the words of the Lord:
For crime after crime of Israel
I will grant them no reprieve,
because they sell the innocent for silver
and destitute for a pair of shoes.
They grind the heads of the poor into the earth
and thrust the humble out of their way.

Micah insisted that all the sacrifices in the world were useless in putting men right with God as long as they persisted in their evil ways.

What shall I bring when I approach the Lord?
How shall I stoop before God in high?
Am I to approach him with whole-offerings or yearling calves?
Will the Lord accept thousands of rams
or ten thousand rivers of oil?
Shall I offer my eldest son for my own wrongdoing,
and children for my own sin?

THE MESSIAH

The prophets continued to proclaim their message through the centuries until after the time when the Israelites returned from being held captive in Babylon. Then the voice of prophesy became silent, but a belief grew up that a last and greatest prophet would come at some time in the future to save the people of God from their troubles. Some said that he would be the prophet Elijah, returned to life, others that Elijah would only be a forerunner for a yet greater prophet, who they called the *Messiah* (saviour).

Today at a solemn moment in the Passover festivities Jews throw open their doors to welcome Elijah should he choose to return that day. It would probably be true, however, that the majority of Jews no longer look for the Messiah to come as a particular individual. The true saviour is the whole body of the children of Israel, chosen by God to serve him and if necessary to suffer in his cause.

An unknown prophet, who wrote at the time of the Babylonian captivity described his people as the servant of God. The servant was called, not to special honour, but to suffer on behalf of all men. The time would come, he said, when the people of other nations would realize that Israel was carrying the troubles of others.

He was despised, he shrank from the sight of men,
tormented and humbled by suffering;
we despised him, we held him of no account,
a thing from which men turn away their eyes.
Yet on himself he bore our sufferings,
our torments he endured,
while we counted him smitten by God,
struck down by disease and misery;
but he was pierced for our transgressions,
tortured for our iniquities;
the chastisement he bore is health for us
and by his scourging we are healed.
We had all strayed like sheep,
each of us had gone his own way;
but the Lord laid upon him
the guilt of us all.

THE LATER HISTORY OF THE JEWS

Thus, some 2,500 years ago, the unknown prophet spoke of his people as God's suffering servant. This role has certainly been laid upon them throughout history on a monstrous scale. Within living memory some 5,000,000 Jews were slaughtered by Hitler's Nazis. This was only the last and most frightful event in a long and sad story of persecution and intolerance. Throughout the Christian era Jews have been hounded from one country to another; they have been herded into ghettos; they have been tortured and killed. This persecution has often been carried out in the name of religion. The Jews, it was said, were responsible for the death of Jesus (but see page 108).

The nations of Europe are made up of a great mixture of racial types. Over the centuries different waves of immigrants have become absorbed until they are no longer distinguishable one from another. The Jews, on the other hand, by continuing to observe the Torah and by meeting together for worship, have preserved their identity in a most remarkable way.

Jews are often accused of keeping themselves apart from the life of the nations in which they live. In fact they have enormously enriched European culture. The Jewish contribution to modern movements in art and science in particular have been far out of proportion to their numerical strength. Jews have also taken a lead in industrial, commercial and political life.

So long as things are going well in any country's life the Jews are accepted as valuable members of society. When things begin to go badly, however, people look round to find some group on whom to vent their frustration and anger. Then the Jews—like the coloured community—stand out as an identifiable group. On the personal level this practice of switching the blame is known as 'kicking the cat'. Unfortunately there seem to be times when whole nations need a cat to kick. Thus the Jews were blamed for the Black Death in the 14th Century as they were blamed for the economic collapse of Germany which preceded the rise of Hitler.

The Jews have responded to the treatment which has been meted out to them with astonishing patience and acceptance of suffering. This spirit of Judaism can be illustrated with a story. When a rabbi and his son were out walking one day, they saw a blind beggar. The father gave his son a shilling to put into the beggar's hat. When the boy returned, the father asked him,

"Did you raise your hat to him, son?"
"But he is blind," replied the boy. "He would not see if I did."
"Ah!" said the father. "But he may be an impostor."

Witnesses of the German concentration camps tell how thousands went to their deaths in this spirit. It is, perhaps, natural that there should have been some reaction after the war was over. The Jews who fought their way into Palestine to create the modern state of Israel were most certainly not prepared to accept suffering without doing anything about it. In the bitter relationships in the Middle East today the people of Israel have returned to the older doctrine of 'an eye for an eye and a tooth for a tooth'. This is a natural reaction against generations of persecution, but it is one of the sad ironies of history that their bitterness is turned against Moslem people, who have treated the Jews comparatively well, rather than against the Christians who have treated them so badly.

The 19th Century, Prime Minister Benjamin Disraeli, himself of Jewish stock, once wrote:

The vineyards of Israel have ceased to exist. But the eternal law enjoins the children of Israel still to celebrate the vintage. A race that persists in celebrating their vintage, although they have no fruits to gather, will regain their vineyards.

For generations Jews have greeted each other at Passover time with the words, 'Next year in Jerusalem'. Today they are in Jerusalem, but this has hardly brought in the era of peace which the prophets hoped to see.

Jews all over the world continue to carry out the

regulations, many of which were framed when they were still a nomadic people, and to celebrate the festivals which remind them of the great events of their past. There are no divisions within Judaism of the kind that are found within Christianity, but there is some difference of opinion as to how far the old laws should be modified to take account of the realities of modern living. Orthodox Jews, on the one hand, hold to the letter of the Torah and the Mishnah. Liberal Jews on the other hand, feel that it is necessary to make modifications. All practising Jews, however, believe that it is essential to preserve the identity of the special people of God. They also look to the time when the suffering is complete and God's promise is fulfilled.

Behold, my servant shall prosper,
he shall be lifted up, exalted to the heights.

"Who am I?" asked the Jew. "I am God's servant; but I am not left to serve him on my own. I am an Israelite, a member of the people, chosen by God as his witness on earth."

6
Children of God
CHRISTIANITY

We learn at school that history is divided into two parts. The early years, counted backwards, are labelled B.C.— before Christ. Then we begin to count forward the 'years of Our Lord'—A.D. In Western practice, therefore, history is divided by the event of the birth of Jesus of Nazareth, though it is probable that the traditional dating is a few years out.

As with the Buddha, later writers told of signs and marvels which took place when this great teacher was born. It was said that Mary, his mother,—like the mother of the Buddha—conceived her son in a miraculous way, but it is worth noting that the very earliest Christian scriptures make no mention of this. Christians differ as to how much weight should be given to these birth narratives. All that can be said with reasonable historical certainty is that the child Jesus grew up in Nazareth, a town in the northern part of Palestine, that his parents were relatively poor, and that for the first thirty odd years of his life he did little to draw special attention to himself.

THE ROMAN WORLD

At that time Rome was master of all the lands which bordered on the Mediterranean Sea. The homeland of the Jews, which had in turn been overrun by Assyrians, Babylonians, Persians and Greeks, now lay firmly under the control of her legions. The northern part came within the territory of a puppet ruler, named Herod, while Judea in the south was administered directly by Roman officials.

The beginning of the 1st Century A.D. was a time of religious excitement all over the Empire. The traditional

(opposite) *The head of Mithras, wearing the typical cap*

gods, like Jupiter and Juno, were still honoured in their temples, but people were no longer satisfied with these rather primitive cults and new religions were becoming fashionable, particularly among the soldiers in the army.

From Persia came the worship of Mithras; from Egypt came the cult of Isis and Osiris. These were *mystery religions* with ceremonies and rituals which were kept secret from all but a chosen few. A man or woman to be initiated into Mithras was washed with the blood of a slaughtered bull. The devotee of Isis went through a ceremony designed to unite him with the mythical young king Osiris, who died and rose again from the dead. The important common link of all the mysteries was that they tried to provide men with a way of becoming *at one* with his god.

The Empire, with its many religions, was bound together in the person of the Emperor, who was looked upon as more than a merely human figure. A man could follow the religion of his choice provided he was prepared to offer a sacrifice at the shrine of this great father of all the people. The Jews alone refused to carry out this simple ceremony. Those who did not understand their religion thought that they must be atheists because, not only did they refuse to carry out this act of respect, but they also had no images or gods like other people. The Jews were therefore the only people in the whole Empire who were liable to be persecuted for their religion. Their chief priests were in a particularly difficult situation. On the one side they had to keep on good terms with the Roman authorities, while on the other they had to remain faithful to the traditions of their people.

There were many in Palestine in those early years of the 1st Century who disapproved of the compromises which the priests were forced to make. They remembered the old belief that a redeemer would appear in Israel, and looked for a political Messiah who would save his people from the Romans. It was a time of excitement and expectancy; a time when the slightest spark might set the land alight with rebellion.

THE BEGINNING OF JESUS' MINISTRY

For four centuries the voice of prophecy had been silent
(see page 90-1). Then, some time before the year 30 A.D.
people began to talk of a man called John, who was
preaching in the desert land near the river Jordan. He had
the uncompromising manner and outspoken message which
seemed to mark him out as a prophet in the old tradition.
His message was that the people of his generation must
repent, leave their wicked ways and return to God. He
called men to come to the river and there receive a token

The Church of the Nativity, Bethlehem

washing, or *baptism*, as a sign of the forgiveness of their sins. As John preached the mood of excitement grew more and more intense. Some said that Elijah had at last returned to his people. God was intervening in the affairs of the children of Israel, as he had intervened to lead them out of Egypt. The Romans would soon be driven out of Palestine, and the new age of the Kingdom of God would be brought in.

Then one day Jesus appeared among the crowds at the river Jordan.

It happened at this time that Jesus came from Nazareth in Galilee and was baptized in the Jordan by John. At the moment when he came up out of the water, he saw the heavens torn open and the Spirit, like a dove, descending upon him. And a voice spoke from heaven: 'Thou art my Son, my Beloved; on thee my favour rests.'

This is the moment that Mark, the earliest of the gospel writers, chooses to begin his narrative of the life of Jesus—the moment when he was singled out as a special instrument of God's purpose. Was this the Messiah that the Jews had expected? The New Testament writers do not answer that question as clearly as might have been expected. Jesus was *Christos*, the anointed one, but he was a very different kind of saviour from the one that everyone expected.

We have seen (page 47) that in the moment of his enlightenment the Buddha was subject to the assaults of Mara, the tempter, Jesus had to pass through a similar spiritual experience before he was able to begin his preaching. He went alone into the wilderness where, for 40 days and nights, his mission was tested out by Satan. Only after he had survived this ordeal, did he return to civilization and choose the first members of the little band of disciples who were to stay close to him through his short ministry.

THE TEACHING OF JESUS

If we want to find the words of Jesus we have to turn to the first three gospels which, in the order in which they were written, were, Mark, Luke and Matthew. The fourth gospel of John should probably be looked on more as a meditation on Jesus's teaching than as an account of his life, though it is certainly possible that it contains some original material not in the other three. These gospel accounts have been studied more minutely than any other historical documents. The earliest was written a generation after Jesus died; the latest possibly some 40 years after that. Many Christians believe that every word they record is absolutely accurate, but most scholars think that the original kernel of Jesus' message has to be understood through several layers of later additions. Conclusions cannot be reached with absolute certainty and there are many who say that it is wrong to study sacred writings with such critical eyes. The scholars have, however, helped us to understand the essential message of Jesus. We may look at it under three headings:— the Kingdom, the Law and the Nature of God.

The Kingdom
Mark tells us that, when Jesus came out of the wilderness, he immediately started preaching this message;

The time has come;
The Kingdom of God is upon you;
Repent and believe the Gospel (good news).

He was therefore telling his countrymen that their long wait was over. God, who had sometimes seemed far away during the years of hardship, had broken into their national story once again and would now establish his kingdom on earth. Jesus presented his message as a Jew to the Jews. Every sabbath he went into the synagogues. The people realized that this teacher had something new to say, so he was asked to read the holy books and expound them to the congregation. Luke tells how he proclaimed his message in his own home town.

So he came to Nazareth, where he had been brought up, and went to synagogue on the Sabbath day as he regularly did. He stood up to read the lesson and was handed the scroll of the prophet Isaiah. He opened the scroll and found the passage which says,
'The spirit of the Lord is upon me because he has annointed me;
He has sent me to announce good news to the poor,
to proclaim release for prisoners and recovery of sight
for the blind;
to let the broken victims go free,
to proclaim the year of the Lord's favour.'
He rolled up the scroll, gave it back to the attendant, and sat down; and all eyes in the synagogue were fixed on him.
He began to speak: 'Today,' he said, 'in your very hearing this text has come true.'

The good news of the coming of the kingdom could not have been more clearly spelt out. At first the people were impressed, but then they remembered that the young man who was making such large claims had grown up among them. They therefore turned on him and tried to throw him over a cliff.

It is easy enough to say that Jesus preached the coming of the kingdom of God; it is much harder to understand just what he meant. We may start with one negative point. Jesus did not announce the arrival of a political kingdom which would overthrow Roman rule in Palestine. On one occasion some enemies, trying to draw him into treason against the authorities, asked him a leading question.

'Are we or are we not permitted to pay taxes to the Roman Emperor? Shall we pay or not?' He saw how crafty their question was, and said, 'Why are you trying to catch me out? Fetch me a silver piece, and let me look at it.' They brought one, and he said to them, 'Whose head is this, and whose inscription?' 'Caesar's,' they replied. Then Jesus said, 'Pay Caesar what is due to Caesar, and pay God what is due to God.'

He was quite clearly saying that the Jewish people owed obedience to Rome. No doubt many of those who had hoped great things of him felt bitterly let down.

The second point that we must make about Jesus' view of the kingdom was that he thought that the world was on the brink of immense and shattering events that would bring in the final day of the Lord, which would usher in the last phase of the earth's existence. First there would be earthquakes, bloodshed and confusion. Then the great events would take place.

But in those days, after that distress, the sun will be darkened, the moon will not give her light; the stars will come falling from the sky, the celestial powers will be shaken. Then they will see the Son of Man coming in the clouds with great power and glory, and he will send out the angels and gather his chosen from the four winds, from the farthest bounds of earth to the farthest bounds of heaven.

These events, he said, were due to take place within the lifetime of some of those who followed him. In later years, when the first generation of Christians had died off and the Son of Man had not come with power, people decided that Jesus must have been referring to the events which led up to the destruction of the Temple by the Romans. Yet it seems impossible to deny that Jesus himself felt that he lived on the brink of an even greater catastrophe.

If we read the Gospels carefully, however, we find that Jesus did not just look on the kingdom as something which would come in world shaking power. Although most men could not recognize it, it had in one sense already come. If men wanted to find the kingdom all they had to do was to look into their own hearts.

"Where is the kingdom?" "How can I find it?" We can imagine the people who crowded round Jesus asking the same questions over and over again. But Jesus shared something of that dislike of abstract questioning that we saw in the Buddha. He therefore answered the questions with concrete images and stories drawn from nature and the everyday world of common folk. The kingdom is like a seed, which starts as something tiny and grows into a great tree. The kingdom is like a thief, creeping up unseen in the night. The kingdom is like a woman who loses one coin from her necklace and cannot rest until she has found it. The parables are like light glancing on the different faces of a crystal. Each gives just a hint of the whole. From them we see that the kingdom is something which works unseen, like yeast in bread, and which makes demands on each individual.

The Law

As a good Jew, Jesus was brought up to respect and to obey all the regulations which were laid down in the Torah and the Mishnah. Yet very early in his ministry he seems to have started to rebel against what he considered to be an excessive respect for mere regulations. On one occasion he healed a man's hand on the Sabbath day. Now the Jewish law was quite clear on the point that healing was work which could only be done on the Sabbath in dire emergency. There was no emergency on this occasion as the hand could just as well have been healed on the following day. On another occasion he was reprimanded for allowing his disciples to pluck ears of corn on the Sabbath. His reply seemed to imply that he had the right to change the law.

'The Sabbath was made for the sake of man and not man for the Sabbath: therefore the Son of Man is sovereign even over the Sabbath.'

On the one hand, therefore, Jesus was a rebel against the traditions of his people. But at the same time he insisted that he had not come to do away with the law but to complete it. What he did was to give it a complete change of emphasis. The direction of this change follows naturally from his view of the kingdom. Men and women had to look for the kingdom of God inside themselves; in the same way they had to find the true law, not in a set of regulations laid down by rabbis, but inside their own hearts.

It needed constant watchfulness and care for any man to keep every regulation of the Torah and the Mishnah, but the task was just about possible. Jesus presented a new law which seemed beyond the power of any man.

You have learned that our forefathers were told, 'Do not commit murder; anyone who commits murder must be brought to judgement.' But what I tell you is this: Anyone who nurses anger against his brother must be brought to judgement. If he abuses his brother he must answer for it to the court; if he sneers at him he will have to answer for it in the fires of hell.

You have learned that they were told, 'Do not commit adultery.' But what I tell you is this: If a man looks on a woman with a lustful eye, he has already committed adultery with her in his heart.

You have learned that they were told, 'Love your neighbour, hate your enemy.' But what I tell you is this: Love your enemies and pray for your persecutors; only so can you be children of your heavenly Father, who makes his sun rise on good and bad alike, and sends the rain on the honest and the dishonest.

The guiding principle of his new law was love; its demands were absolute. The disciple has to be prepared to give up his wealth, and even his family ties if called upon to do so.

An interesting parallel can be drawn between Jesus and the Buddha. Both appeared on the scene at a time when the religion into which they were born had become somewhat set and formalized. In rebelling against this, both threw the responsibility back onto the individual. Of course in time both Buddhism and Christianity became set and formalized in their turn in ways that might well have appalled their founders.

The Nature of God

To the Jews, as we have seen, Jahweh was so holy that he had to be approached with a respect that bordered on fear. Some of the later prophets, however, began to stress the loving nature of God. This loving nature was particularly seen in his relationship with his chosen people. 'When Israel was a child I loved him,' said Hosea, and that prophet compared the love of God with that felt by a husband for an erring wife.

Jesus developed this strain of Hebrew thinking to such an extent that the writer of the Fourth Gospel summed up his teaching about God in the words, 'God is love'. Jews had talked of God as their father, but Jesus gave this term a new meaning. When he taught his disciples to pray, he told them to use the word *Abba*. This was the close and affectionate term used by every Jewish child to his own father. It might best be translated into English as Dad, or even Daddy.

Jesus was therefore saying that, although God was indeed holy, as the Jews had always believed, he was also very close. The characteristic relationship between a child and his father is one of trust and love. If this is true of human relationship, says Jesus, *how much more* must it be true of a relationship with God. A human parent might let his child down, but it is impossible that God should ever let down his children.

Therefore I bid you put away anxious thoughts about food and drink to keep you alive, and clothes to cover your body. Surely life is more than food, the body more than clothes. Look at the birds of the air; they do not sow and reap and store in barns, yet your heavenly Father feeds them. You are worth more than the birds! Is there a man of you who by anxious thought can add a foot to his height? And why be anxious about clothes? Consider how the lilies grow in the fields; they do not work, they do not spin; and yet, I tell you, even Solomon in all his splendour was not attired like one of these. But if that is how God clothes the grass in the fields, which is there today, and tomorrow is thrown on the stove, will he not all the more clothe you? How little faith you have! No, do not ask anxiously, 'What are we to eat? What are we to drink? What shall we wear?'

Jesus therefore gives a new answer to man's question, 'Who am I?' 'You are a child of God,' he might reply. 'This means that as an individual you are infinitely precious. Since God has given you this special love, you must respond by giving back a child-like trust, and extending God's love to every man.' When a Christian talks of his *faith* in God, he is not first and foremost making a statement that God exists. Until recently very few would have doubted that. To a Christian faith means trust—the proper response to the loving fatherhood of God.

THE MIRACLES

Miracles have been attributed to many of the great religious figures. The miracles of Jesus can be divided into two types. There are the acts of healing, both of physical and mental disease, and there are other acts in which he showed power over the forces of nature. There is no need to be too sceptical about the first group, for in our own times it has been clearly shown that there are a number of people who possess special healing powers. The nature miracles pose greater problems for Christians and opinions would differ as to whether Jesus literally walked on the water and changed water into wine. As with the stories about the Buddha, however, (see page 58) these incidents have a religious importance which is more important than their literal truth. As the healing miracles show Jesus to be lord of men's suffering, so the nature miracles show that he is lord of all creation.

The gospel stories make it quite clear that Jesus did not want his miracles to be treated as proof of the truth of his message. They were generally performed quietly and people were told to say nothing about them. The acts of power were signs that the kingdom had arrived, but Jesus wished no man to find faith in God only because he had witnessed a miracle.

THE MISSION OF THE DISCIPLES

A *missionary* religion is one whose members are committed to go out and seek to spread the truth. This is not true of either Hinduism or Judaism. In both people are born into the faith, and it is difficult for an outsider to gain admission. Buddhism, on the other hand, is a missionary religion, and we have seen how King Asoka sent people to carry the faith to new lands.

Christianity had a missionary emphasis from the beginning. The stress on bringing outsiders into the fold is even stronger than in Buddhism since Christians believe that each individual has but one life in which to find the truth. On two occasions Jesus sent out his followers to preach his gospel. Their instructions were to travel light.

Provide no gold, silver, or copper to fill your purse, no pack for the road, no second coat, no shoes, no stick; the worker earns his keep.

On the first occasion the small group of twelve close disciples were sent to preach to the Jews. On the second occasion a larger band of seventy went out to take the message to the Gentiles as well. Even at this early stage Christianity was beginning to burst the bounds of the Judaism in which it had been born.

THE DEATH OF JESUS

Orthodox Jews had good reason to mistrust this teacher who seemed to be undermining the very Torah itself, and the gospel narratives tell how distrust grew between the religious leaders and the followers of the Gallilean. It is important, however, to recognise that the accounts which we have of the trial and death of Jesus are written from a Christian point of view. They certainly present the chief priests and scribes of Judaism as the villains of the piece, who plot to kill Jesus, and finally almost force the Roman governor, Pontius Pilate, to have him crucified.

It is possible that this is what happened, but there are doubts which ought to be taken into consideration. The gospel writers lived and wrote in the Roman Empire, and they wanted to impress its rulers with the respectability of their religion. They must therefore have been very tempted to shift the responsibility for the death of Jesus away from the Romans and onto the Jews. Also we know something of the character of Pilate from other writings and we gather that he was a cruel man who would have thought little of executing the odd Jewish religious leader. If he did try to save Jesus, as the gospels suggest, he may well have done so to spite the Jewish leaders.

The story of the death of Jesus has been told so often that it is not necessary to recount the events. The gospels make it clear that the disciples were puzzled by this strange twist of events. One week before the Passover they had followed Jesus as he entered Jerusalem as a king, come to claim his inheritance. There were signs of the popular enthusiasm which could carry his cause forward on the crest of a wave. They were the proud lieutenants of the Messiah, come to redeem Israel. It was not a part of the Messiah's role to die on a cross.

Jesus, on the other hand, understood what he was doing. It appears that he had decided that the unknown prophet's words about the suffering servant (see page 92) referred to him. He did not face pain and death with any simple heroics, and on the night of the Thursday before Passover he was weighed down by the ordeal which faced him.

On that evening he gathered his followers in a small upper room for one of those solemn meals which lay at the heart of Jewish religion. He went through the time-honoured actions, and then added his own contribution to the ritual.

During supper he took bread, and having said the blessing he broke it and gave it to them, with the words: 'Take this; this is my body.' Then he took a cup, and having offered thanks to God he gave it to them; and they all drank from it. And he said, 'This is my blood, the blood of the covenant, shed for many. I tell you this: never again shall I drink from the fruit of the vine until that day when I drink it new in the kingdom of God.'

He then led his followers outside the city and, in an agony of mind, left them to pray.

Horror and dismay came over him, and he said to them, 'My heart is ready to break with grief; stop here, and stay awake.' Then he went forward a little, threw himself on the ground, and prayed that, if it were possible, this hour might pass him by. 'Abba, Father,' he said, 'all things are possible to thee; take this cup away from me. Yet not what I will, but what thou wilt.'

Still the disciples were bewildered and puzzled, and they were unprepared to cope with the events which followed so swiftly. Jesus was arrested and taken for trial. According to the narrative the proceedings were taken with unseemly haste so that the execution could be carried out before the Passover festival on the Saturday.

Crucifixion was the standard method by which the Romans disposed of low grade criminals. It was a slow, lingering death by exposure, and Jesus' three hour period of suffering was unusually brief. It is unlikely that the execution of one more religious leader caused very much of a stir at the time. It was a painful and undignified end to a very brief ministry. With the small band of men and women who had followed him scattered and demoralized, it seemed that the last had been heard of the Gallilean.

The Resurrection

We have had cause to note the difference between *historical* and *religious* statements. The crucifixion comes into both categories. There can be little doubt that a teacher called Jesus of Nazareth was executed by Pontius Pilate. But three of the gospels (the earliest versions of Mark end with the death of Jesus) go on to tell how Jesus rose from the dead on the Sunday after the Passover. There has been a great deal of argument as to whether this can also be treated as a historical as well as a religious statement.

Those who say that it can point out that it is very difficult to see how the disciples could have made up such a story. Jewish tradition did not lead them to expect a Messiah who would die and rise again. They ask how such a demoralized band could have been transformed into the dynamic missionaries of the early church unless they were convinced of the truth of what they taught.

Those who argue on the other side point out that the idea of a dying and a rising king was well known in the ancient world (see page 98), even if it was not a part of the Jewish tradition. They also draw attention to the fact that the three gospel accounts of the Resurrection conflict with each other in several important details.

If a historian were asked to pass judgement he might reply that those who argue for the historical accuracy of the Resurrection narrative make out a good case, but, *simply on the grounds of the evidence*, it must fall short of proof. Most Christian scholars are happy to accept this. A believer is challenged to acknowledge the resurrection of Christ with his heart and not with his head. Jesus, indeed, said as much to Thomas.

'Reach your finger here; see my hands. Reach your hand here and put it into my side. Be unbelieving no longer, but believe.' Thomas said, 'My Lord and my God!' Jesus said, 'Because you have seen me you have found faith. Happy are they who never saw me and yet have found faith.'

The resurrection of Christ is therefore a religious statement. It lies at the heart of the Christian faith. Like Judaism, Christianity is a historical religion, founded on events which took place at a specific moment in history. Yet Christians have always believed that with the resurrection Jesus broke through the barrier of time.

If two words had to be chosen to represent the essential message of Christianity, they could be, *Jesus lives*. Immense structures of Christian theology and piety have been built on this central statement. In his teaching Jesus told his disciples that they were children of God. By the resurrection he gave a pledge that the believer would never be left alone. Matthew sums this up in the words with which he ended his gospel. 'Be assured, I am with you, to the end of time.'

The resurrection is remembered by Christians every year at Easter time. Hints of ancient pagan rites still cling to this festival. The very name of Easter comes from Eastri, the pagan goddess of the dawn. This is the spring festival of new life, the time when Persephone left the underworld where she had spent the winter months. Churches are decorated with the flowers of spring. But to Christians these are just symbols of that more important new life into which they are born with Christ.

The Christian doctrine of a future life is based more on the event of Christ's resurrection than on the words of his teaching. Certainly he accepted the general belief of his time that after death men would come face to face with the judgement of a holy God. The sheep would be set at God's right hand to share the joys of heaven; the goats would be cast into outer darkness where there would be weeping and wailing and grinding of teeth. Yet Jesus saw the kingdom of God as something immediate—something which breaks into the living experience of human beings. He can hardly, therefore, be accused of preaching 'pie in the sky when you die'.

Christians, however, believe that Christ's resurrection sets the seal on the promise that the human life is not just bounded by birth on the one hand and death on the other.

Jesus lives! No longer now
Can thy sting O death enthrall us.

The ancient Easter hymns stress the belief that the resurrection is the pledge of immortality for those whose lives are joined to the life of Christ.

Pentecost

Forty days separate the Jewish festivals of Passover and Pentecost. The gospels report that during that period Jesus made a number of resurrection appearances to his disciples before finally being taken up into heaven. On the day of Pentecost the disciples met in a house in Jerusalem and there underwent an experience of dramatic power. Telling the story in his book of Acts, Luke describes how tongues of fire came upon them and they began to speak in all kinds of different languages.

Ecstatic experiences of this kind are common to many religions. There are well authenticated accounts of people who handle poisonous snakes without fear or lose all sense of pain when they are in the grip of a powerful religious emotion. In this way at Pentecost the power of God—the *Holy Ghost*—came on the disciples. They rushed out into the street, and behaved in a way that made passers-by think that they were drunk. Insisting that they were sober, Peter began to preach the first Christian sermon. His words provided the basis for the earliest teaching of the church. Firstly he proclaimed the facts of the life and death of Jesus.

'Men of Israel, listen to me: I speak of Jesus of Nazareth, a man singled out by God and made known to you through miracles, portents, and signs, which God worked among you through him, as you well know. When he had been given up to you, by the deliberate will and plan of God, you used heathen men to crucify and kill him. But God raised him to life again, setting him free from the pangs of death, because it could not be that death should keep him in its grip.'

He went on to show how these events were in line with the Jewish expectation of the coming of a saviour. Then he ended with a challenge.

'Repent, repent and be baptized, every one of you, in the name of Jesus the Messiah for the forgiveness of your sins; and you will receive the gift of the Holy Spirit.'

THE EARLY CHURCH

At Jerusalem the believers centred round the dominating figure of Peter. For a time they organized their lives on a communal basis, pooling all their possessions. But when hard times came these Jerusalem Christians were reduced to the brink of starvation. Other Christian communities therefore did not follow their example of rejecting private property. Each local community of believers was known as a *church*.

Those early Christians possessed a fierce enthusiasm which carried them through waves of persecution. Among their most bitter enemies was a Jewish rabbi called Saul of Tarsus. The Book of Acts tells the well known story of how he was converted to become the spearhead of the Christian missionary thrust. The word *conversion* literally means a turning round; the conversion of Paul is one of the most dramatic turnings round in history. Before his experience on the Damascus Road he had thought entirely as a Jew. Afterwards he became the man responsible for interpreting the new Christian gospel to the educated Greeks and Romans of his day. He rejected the law more completely than Jesus himself had done and presented Christianity as a faith for people of all races and cultural backgrounds. It was he who carried the teaching across the Straits of Bosphorus, so that for the first time in history a major religion began to spread in Europe.

WHAT DOES IT MEAN?

Paul had a logical and highly trained mind. When he set out to interpret the life and teaching of Jesus he therefore had to face up to the hard question—'What does it mean?' He explored this problem in a series of letters written to the members of different churches. Scholars do not agree about how many of the epistles which carry his name were actually written by the Apostle, but some of those which were probably written by others still reflect his thought.

For Paul the essential message of Christ lies, not in his teaching, important though that was, but in the great actions of his death and resurrection. In attempting to answer the question, 'Why did Jesus die?' Paul lays the basis of the religious thinking, which is known as *theology*. His argument must be summarized briefly, and somewhat crudely.

In his natural state, says Paul, man is separated from God. However hard he tries to be good he finds that evil creeps into his actions. The Jews had tried to overcome this natural tendency to sin by observing the instructions of the Torah and the Mishnah to the letter. But, argues the ex-rabbi, their labour is in vain, for, however hard they try, the gulf which divides man from God remains unbridged.

I discover this principle, then: that when I want to do the right, only the wrong is within my reach. In my inmost self I delight in the law of God, but I perceive that there is in my bodily members a different

law, fighting against the law that my reason approves and making me
a prisoner under the law that is in my members, the law of sin.

We have seen that in many religions man makes himself
at one with his gods by offering them a sacrifice. While the
Temple stood the Chief Priest offered sacrifice for the
people on the Day of Atonement. The Christian has no
such sacrifice to offer. He is therefore helpless and unable
to get himself out of his predicament. But in the death of
Christ God took the initiative and offered his own son as a
sacrifice for men. Here then is the answer to the question,
'Who is there to rescue me?'

God alone, through Jesus Christ our Lord! Thanks be to God! In a
word then, I myself, subject to God's law as a rational being, am yet,
in my unspiritual nature, a slave to the law of sin.

Paul proclaimed that at-one-ment with God comes through
Christ's sacrifice on the Cross. By this act the old
judgement for sin is taken away.

The conclusion of the matter is this: there is no condemnation for
those who are united with Christ Jesus, because in Christ Jesus the
life-giving law of the Spirit has set you free from the law of sin and
death.

Mark, who was a companion of Paul on his travels
expressed this in vivid pictorial language, which should
probably be read as a parable rather than a statement of
historical fact. At the end of his gospel he wrote that, in
the moment that Jesus died on the cross 'the curtain of the
Temple was torn in two from top to bottom.' This was the
curtain which shut men out from the holiest of holies,
where the glory of God resided. After the sacrifice of
Christ there could no longer be any such division.
Henceforth God would dwell among man.
   The initiative in redeeming man therefore lay with God.
As he had intervened to save his people when they came
out of Egypt, so he intervened again. But now, says Paul,

there has been a change. The old Israel was the Hebrew tribe which inherited the law given on Mount Sinai. The new Israel consists of all those people, of whatever nationality they might be, who respond to God's love by placing their trust in Christ's sacrifice. It is on these terms that a man or woman can come into that very close relationship with God of which Jesus had spoken.

For all who are moved by the Spirit of God are sons of God. The Spirit you have received is not a spirit of slavery leading you back into a life of fear, but a Spirit that makes us sons, enabling us to cry, 'Abba! Father!' In that cry the Spirit of God joins with out spirit in testifying that we are God's children; and if children, then heirs. We are God's heirs and Christ's fellow-heirs, if we share his suffering now in order to share his splendour hereafter.

The Trinity

Scholars disagree about when the last of the books which make up the New Testament were written. Some time early in the 1st Century the Christian scriptures were complete. Together with the older Jewish writings they made up the Bible which formed the foundation of Christian belief. A number of problems, however, still remained.

The most serious of these centred around the person of Jesus. Christianity grew out of monotheistic Judaism, with its central statement, 'Hear Oh Israel, the Lord our God, the Lord is One.' When talking about himself Jesus most commonly used the ambiguous phrase, 'the Son of Man'. Yet the New Testament writings made it clear that Jesus was God as well as man.

For the divine nature was his from the first; yet he did not think to snatch at equality with God, but made himself nothing, assuming the nature of a slave. Bearing the human likeness, revealed in human shape, he humbled himself, and in obedience accepted even death—death on a cross. Therefore God raised him to the heights and bestowed on him the name above all names, that at the name of Jesus every knee should bow—in heaven, on earth, and in the depths—and every tongue confess, 'Jesus Christ is Lord', to the glory of God the Father.

The New Testament also spoke of the Holy Spirit which came on the disciples at Pentecost as being in a real sense God.

Christians were therefore left with something of a puzzle. As heirs to the Jewish tradition, they could not believe in three gods, but at the same time they could not water down the Bible by reducing the status of Jesus. During the first centuries of the Christian era there were long drawn out and bitter disputes while the church tried to work out an acceptable formula which would cover both points. Some of the quarrels seem very petty to modern eyes. A great split occurred on one occasion over a single letter in one word of a formula. One side wanted to say that Christ was of *like* substance with the father; the other that he was of the *same* substance with the father. It is not easy for us to understand what the dispute was all about unless we first study some Greek philosophy to discover what they meant by the word 'substance'! Yet behind all the bickering important principles were at stake.

Out of these long disputes emerged the Christian doctrine of the Trinity. There is one God, it affirms, but within this one God are three persons—Father, Son and Holy Spirit. We have seen that Hindus and Buddhists are prepared to leave a great deal to the individual in what he chooses to believe or disbelieve. Christians, on the other hand, from very early times reduced the essentials of their faith to formulations, or *creeds,* which every believer was obliged to accept. The simplest of these is the Apostles' Creed, which talks of Christ in terms used by the New Testament. The two later Nicene and Athanasian Creeds analyse the nature of Christ in much more complex terms. By reading the latter it is possible to catch an echo of the bitter disputes which raged in the early church. Christ is, it declares,

God of the substance of the Father, begotten before the worlds; and Man of the substance of his mother, born in the world. Perfect God and perfect Man; of a reasonable soul and human flesh subsisting . . . One; not by conversion of the Godhead into flesh; but by taking of the Godhead into flesh, but by taking of the Manhood into God;

One altogether; not by confusion of the substance, but by the unity of person.

THE CHURCH

We have seen (page 113) that the word 'church' was used in the New Testament to describe a group of Christians gathered together in a particular place. In much the same way that Jewish synagogues had rabbis, these Christian communities had recognized *presbyters* to act as spiritual guides and teachers. By about a century after the death of Christ it appears to have become common that the senior presbyter should be called a *bishop*.

It was natural that before long these individual churches should begin to group themselves together into a larger organization. At the eastern end of the Mediterranean Sea the bishops of Jerusalem, Antioch, and Constantinople became recognized as patriarchs. Further west the influence of the bishop of Rome spread rapidly. His church had a special claim to primacy, since it held the key position in the capital city of the Empire and it could claim that it had been founded by the Apostle Peter himself.

In this way the fragmented churches began to come together into one organization, which can be described as the church. The *clergy*, who were set apart to minister to the needs of the faithful, were no longer responsible only to their own flock. Henceforth they were appointed by and answerable to the bishops and patriarchs who were set over them. The church had by this time become an institution, with its own rules and discipline.

The Sacraments

At the centre of the church's existence was its regular and ordered worship. There were different forms of service for many occasions, but from the beginning the central acts of worship of the church were the two great sacraments of baptism and the eucharist, which could be traced back to the commands of Christ himself. A *sacrament* contains a religious action which has a special symbolism attached to it.

We have seen (page 100) that Jesus himself accepted *baptism* at the hands of John and that immediately after Pentecost Peter went out into the streets of Jerusalem to preach baptism for the forgiveness of sins (page 113). The religious action in baptism is a washing with water. The symbolism of this action is that at that moment the individual dies to his old sinful life and is born again to a new life in Christ. In the early days of the church only adults who understood what they were doing could be baptised. It was, however, generally believed that only those who had been baptised could be saved in the day of judgement. It was therefore natural that before long Christian parents should seek baptism for their children, and infant baptism has been commonly practised through the centuries.

The *eucharist* is the sacrament in which the church remembers Christ's sacrifice on the cross. The actions are those which Jesus performed at the meal which he took with his disciples on the Thursday before that last Passover of his life. Paul placed it on record in a letter how from the earliest times Christians relived that most sacred time by obeying Christ's instructions to do as he had done.

For the tradition which I handed on to you came to me from the Lord himself: that the Lord Jesus, on the night of his arrest, took bread and after giving thanks to God, broke it and said: 'This is my body, which is for you; do this as a memorial of me.' In the same way, he took the cup after supper, and said: 'This cup is the new covenant sealed by my blood. Whenever you drink it, do this as a memorial of me.' For every time you eat this bread and drink this cup, you proclaim the death of the Lord, until he comes.

The eucharist has taken many forms under many different names in different branches of the Christian church, but the essential actions, the essential words have remained the same. Again, Christians have differed, and at times have

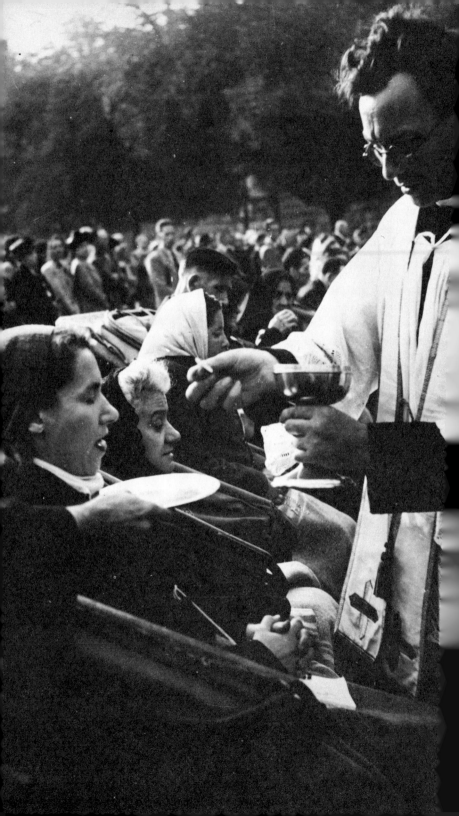

persecuted each other unmercifully over the meaning of this action.

Baptism and the eucharist are the only two sacraments which can be traced back to Christ's command. Both the Roman Catholic and Eastern Orthodox churches, however, recognize five other sacraments. These are confirmation, marriage, the last unction, penance and the ordination of clergy.

MONASTICISM

We have seen (page 62) that from the earliest times Buddhists who wanted to follow the path of enlightenment joined the sangha. Unlike the Buddha, Jesus did not himself found any order of monks. In the early centuries of the church's life, however, individuals withdrew from society and cut themselves off from the cares and distractions of family life in order to devote themselves to religion. The earliest of these holy men lived alone in cells or caves as *hermits*. In time, however, they gathered together to live in communities which were known as monasteries. Even holy men need some measure of organization when they try to live together, and at various times great individuals have drawn up codes of discipline, which were adopted as the *rule* of life for generations of monks. In the Western Church (see pages 128-133) there have been many different orders of monks; each order following a different rule.

It is hard for those who enjoy their day to day life in the world to understand why so many millions of men and women over the ages should voluntarily have shut themselves up to live a life of sacrifice and self-discipline. Those who defend the monastic life put forward two basic reasons.

In the first place the Christian monk, like his Buddhist opposite number in Theravada countries, seeks to work

(opposite) *The sacrament of Eucharist (Holy Communion) administered in the open air*

In the Vatican City, nuns work on the restoration of arrases and tapestries

out his own salvation. Every generation has its own special brand of evil, and it is hard to live in the world and remain untainted. A monk's life was so full that he had little opportunity for sin, except perhaps for sins of thought. It has therefore been widely believed that a monk had a better chance of getting to heaven than had a layman.

But monks do not shut themselves away just so that they can follow a private road to heaven. Every individual has his function to perform for the benefit of society as a whole. While other men work at their various occupations, the monk prays for his fellow men. In the most famous of all monastic rules the monk's day was divided into three parts. 8 hours were spent in worship, 8 hours in work and 8 hours in sleeping and eating. In practice monks often spend more than the prescribed 8 hours in worship. Through the centuries the daily services have been sung in countless monasteries, starting with prime in the small hours of the morning and ending with compline last thing in the evening. Individual monks come and go, but the services go on from one century to another. The monks pray on behalf of all the busy people who have little time to pray. Over the centuries simple peasants, working in the fields, have paused when they heard the monastery bell and remembered that the monks would be approaching God on their behalf.

THE CONVERSION OF CONSTANTINE

In the early centuries the church had to face bitter persecution, and at times it was driven underground to become almost a secret society.

In the year 312 A.D., however, the picture changed completely. It was said that when the Emperor Constantine was riding through France one day he looked up into the sky and saw a cross of light over the sun, with the words, 'In this sign conquer'. At that moment he became a Christian, and he made Christianity the religion of the state. Since that time, except for a few comparatively brief interludes, Europe has been a Christian continent. It is perhaps a strange twist of history that the faith based on the life and teaching of Jesus of Nazareth should have become the official creed of one of the world's most violent civilizations. Jesus had proclaimed that the poor would inherit the earth, but after the conversion of Constantine the church has often worked for the benefit of the rich and the powerful.

THE DIVISION OF THE CHURCH

By the time of the break up of the Roman Empire the quarrels between different sections of opinion within the church were already hardening into definite *schism*, or division. The Semitic people of the eastern Mediterranean broke away during the disputes on the nature of Christ. Today there are small but ancient Christian communities

in Persia, Armenia, Syria, Ethiopia and India, which do not
share the creeds accepted by other Christians.

Constantine himself was indirectly responsible for the
second great schism. After becoming a Christian he
decided to leave Rome and set up his capital at Constantinople. Later the empire was divided into a Greek half,
based on Constantinople, and a Latin half, based on Rome.
As these two drifted apart, the Greek and the Latin
churches began to lose contact with one another. The final
split came in the year 1054 A.D., when a Roman cardinal
walked into the great church of St. Sophia in Constantinople and placed a bull of excommunication on the altar.
Both parties claimed that the other had cut itself from
the one true church.

For centuries the Bishops of Rome, who were known as
papa, (father), or *pope*, had been gathering more and more
power into their own hands, until they had effective
control in the West. Believing, however, that they were
rightly rulers over the whole church, popes tried to extend
their authority in the East as well. Greek Christians were
prepared to treat the Pope as the senior bishop, but they
would not agree that he had any right to issue orders. They
therefore rejected the Pope's claims.

If the Holy Pontiff, seated on the lofty throne of his glory, wishes
to thunder at us and, so to speak, hurl his mandates at us from on
high, and if he wishes to judge us and even to rule us and our
Churches, not by taking counsel with us but at his own arbitrary
pleasure, what kind of brotherhood can this be? We should be the
slaves, not the sons, of such a church.

THE EASTERN ORTHODOX CHURCH

The Orthodox Church was based on the Eastern Roman
Empire, which continued in existence until the Turks
captured Constantinople in 1453 A.D. By that time it had
also extended north into Russia. Today the Eastern church
has two main branches, the Russian and the Greek. There
is no single head of the church, but it has preserved a

fundamental unity based on the two pillars of ortho-doxy—right belief and right worship.

Eastern Christians believe that they have preserved the true message of the faith, while Western Christians, be they Catholic or Protestant, have brought in new and undesirable elements. They base their *right beliefs* on the agreements which were reached by the bishops of the early church when they met together in General Councils.

Except in one small, and comparatively speaking, insignificant point, the creeds of the Eastern and the Western church are identical, but over the years the two communions have placed their emphasis in different places. Western Christians, for instance, have tended to lay a great deal of stress on Christ's suffering on the Cross. Those from the East, on the other hand, refuse to separate the Crucifixion and the Resurrection. The person they worship on the Cross is Christ in glory, not Jesus in pain. 'I call him king, because I see him crucified,' said an early Eastern saint. This is the cornerstone of orthodox belief.

When we use the word 'belief' in Western Europe we are generally referring to the action of accepting something with our brains. Thus when a Western Christian says 'I believe' he is giving intellectual assent to the statements which the creed contains. The further east you go the less this is true. We have seen that Hindus and Buddhists care little about belief in this sense. Eastern Christians are certainly more concerned about what they believe than are Hindus or Buddhists, but they would still insist that right belief cannot be a thing of the brain alone, but must spring out of *right worship*. Before the creed is recited in an Orthodox Church the priest turns to his people and says,

Let us love one another, that with one mind we may confess Father, Son and Holy Spirit, Trinity one in essence and undivided.

So it is only in the unity of the church that the Christian can recite the creed.

The Orthodox Church is first and foremost a worshipping community. It is more than a thousand years since eastern scholars did any startlingly new thinking about their beliefs, and preaching has virtually disappeared from their services. But year after year, week after week, the great *liturgies* (forms of service) of Basil and Chrystostom, the early fathers of the church, are repeated in unhurried and solemn fashion. Eastern Christians claim that their worship can give each individual Christian a vision of the supernatural world, which lies far beyond his daily experience.

The worshipper is called upon to use all the senses of his body. The words of the liturgy are but a part of the whole, rich experience. His ears can listen to the traditional music, while the heavy smell of incense lingers in his nose. All the time his eyes are beguiled with a pageantry of colour and movement.

The mysteries of the Eucharist itself are performed by priests behind a solid wooden screen, which divides the holy place from the body of the congregation. The screen is covered with a mass of *ikons* (religious pictures), which show a vast company of saints who can help the individual in his or her approach to God. In early days there were bitter disputes between those who wanted to sweep the churches clear of these ikons, and those who believed that they were an important part of the Orthodox tradition. In the end the latter party won the day. These pictures are looked upon as more than mere visual aids to help in worship. In the words of one writer.

The ikon is a song of triumph, a revelation, and an enduring monument to the victory of the saints and the disgrace of the demons.

Monasticism has always played an important part in the life of the Eastern Church. In early centuries holy men who competed to out-do one another in acts of asceticism, were held in great reverence by simple folk. Since the 10th Century the centre of Eastern monasticism has been Mount Athos, on the Black Sea, where there are 20 large monasteries, besides smaller ones and a number of hermits' cells. When it was at its most flourishing no less than 40,000 monks lived on the one mountain.

The ordinary parish priests are normally men of peasant

stock, who are close to the people they serve. They are allowed to marry and raise children in the normal way. The bishops, who rule the church, are not recruited from the ranks of these lower clergy, but from the monasteries, and are expected to live a single life.

In Orthodox countries there has never been a sharp division between church and state. Constantine's successors in the office of Emperor were looked upon as the representatives of Christ on earth, and this tradition was inherited by the Tsars of Russia. On the other side bishops have not been averse to engaging in politics, and in our own time the prime minister of Cyprus is an Archbishop of the Greek church. In the days when the British ruled the island he took a leading part in his country's struggle for

These three monks of St. Barnabas Monastery, near Famagusta, are painters of Ikons, an important part of the Orthodox tradition

independence.

This close link between church and state has had unexpected consequences in Eastern Europe, for, when the communists turned on the Tsarist Empire in Russia, they naturally attacked the church which had supported it for so long. Russian communism is bitterly anti-Christian. Teachers are instructed to root out any sign of religion in the children in their charge. During Stalin's time many were persecuted and the church had to go underground, as in the early Christian centuries. This is how one Russian described their worship during those years.

> The Easter service was held in an apartment of an official state institution. Entrance was possible only with a special pass, which I obtained for myself and for my small daughter. About thirty people were present, among them some of my acquaintances. An old priest celebrated the service, which I shall never forget. 'Christ is risen', we sang softly, but full of joy . . . The joy that I felt in this service of the catacomb church gives me strength to live, even today.

It can hardly be denied that the Russian Church had at times served as an instrument of oppression. But the Communist leaders were mistaken in thinking that they would be able to sweep it aside. Today many millions of Russians, particularly from the humbler ranks of society, continue to worship in the ancient liturgies of Orthodoxy. The power of the Eastern Church lies in its overriding emphasis on worship. Through this the individual is able to feel himself a part of an unchanging community which exists to adore its risen Lord.

THE WESTERN CATHOLIC CHURCH

Eastern Christians believe that the church has only one head, and that is Christ himself. He gave the care of his flock to the apostles, who in their turn passed it on to bishops who succeeded each other through the generations. At the time of the split between the Greek and the Latin churches the Pope in Rome was setting out a different theory. Christ, indeed, founded the church, but he then chose one of his disciples to take his place after he had ascended into heaven. Simon was one of the earliest disciples to be chosen, and Jesus renamed him Peter—or rock. 'You are Peter,' said Jesus, 'and on this rock I will build my church'. According to the papal argument, therefore, all the power that Jesus had held when he was on earth had devolved onto the Apostle. In time Peter became bishop of Rome. After Peter had been killed by the Roman authorities his special position as head of the church and representative of Christ on earth was inherited by his successors as bishop of Rome.

The church had long held that Christ was *infallible*—that is, he was unable to make a mistake. It followed from this that the pope was also infallible. We must, however, be careful about how we interpret this. The Roman Church has never claimed that every pope is perfect, or that every utterance he makes has the authority of Christ. What it does claim is that, when a pope makes a clear and definite statement on behalf of the Church as a whole, then he speaks with the voice of Christ himself.

Eastern Christians criticised the Western church for introducing new doctrines which were not to be found in the Bible or in the early church. They therefore claimed that the pope was no longer orthodox. Popes replied to this charge by insisting that the church had the right to declare new doctrines. Jesus had promised to lead his disciples 'into all truth'. This implied that there were truths which had not at that time been revealed. These would be opened up in the fullness of time.

The 'doctrine of development can be strikingly illustrated from the beliefs which have in the course of the centuries surrounded the person of Mary, mother of Jesus. In the New Testament writings she figures, when at all, as a comparatively unimportant character. Then in the early Christian centuries she grew in importance and the cult of the Virgin Mary, Mother of God, began to flourish.

Hebrew religion had always had a very masculine emphasis. God is referred to as 'he'; the prophets and the looked for Messiah were all male. But for centuries the Mediterranean people had worshipped mother goddesses which brought warmth and the promise of fertility to their lives. With the rise of the cult of the Virgin all these emotions could be turned to the worship of the Mother of God. In time the doctrine of the Virgin became part of the established doctrine of the church. Like her son, she was said to be born without sin (the immaculate conception). At the end of her life she did not die, like other folk, but was taken up bodily into heaven. It was impossible to claim that these doctrines were laid down in the Bible. They have, however, been proclaimed by an infallible Pope, speaking on behalf of the whole church and Catholics are duty bound to accept them.

The bishops of Rome established their authority at a time when princes and nobles were struggling for power in Western Europe. Had they failed to do so the church would have become subordinate to these secular rulers. But strong minded popes insisted that the clergy's allegiance to the church came before their allegiance to the state. Bishops and priests were forbidden to marry so that they should not be tempted to gather riches and lands which they could pass on to their children. Where the ordinary clergy were too much under the power of the secular rulers, the popes used monks as agents of their policy.

By about the 13th Century the popes had welded the Western Church into a cohesive and immensely powerful organisation. It remains today, by a very long way, the largest and most closely knit religious institution in the world. From top to bottom it is based on the principle of obedience. The Pope takes pride in his title of 'servant of the servants of God'. He is called upon to rule this immense organization in obedience to the will of God. Below him there is a pyramid of cardinals, archbishops, bishops and lower clergy, each with his appointed place in the heirarchy.

The individual layman is born into this church at baptism. He receives God's grace at the great milestones of his life—confirmation, matrimony, death—through the sacraments of the church. If he has sinned he must go to a priest and make a formal act of penance before he can find forgiveness.

Some people have asked whether a mariner could continue to be a Catholic when shipwrecked on a desert island. Catholics would reply that man was not created to live as an isolated animal, and God could no doubt give special grace in such special circumstances. For the normal circumstances of human life God chooses to come to man by way of his church and its seven sacraments. Six of these sacraments are reserved for special occasions, but the Eucharist, or the Mass, as it is known to Catholics, provides a regular means of grace, available to all the faithful.

Catholic priests celebrate Mass each day of their lives, and on Sundays the Mass is the central service in every church. Without this sacrament the church would cease to exist, for Catholics believe that it is on the altar that Christ gives himself to his people. When the priest consecrates the bread and the wine, these elements *become* the body and blood of Christ. Again, we must be careful how we understand this. Many simple believers understand this change in very crude terms. Theologians, however, have taught that the outward form of the bread and the wine remains the same, while the change takes place on a deeper spiritual level. However it is explained, it remains central to Catholic thinking that there is a change and God comes to his people in a real and indeed a bodily form when the priests repeats the words which were spoken at the last supper.

To the Catholic, therefore, the institution of the church is inseparable from his religion. The Pope occupies Christ's place on earth, and the sacraments provide channels for his grace to come to the individual believer. This individual believer has to renounce his freedom to pick and choose what he will and will not believe. In return he is able to find reassurance from the anxieties and stresses of life. Every priest is his father; the church is his mother. The

Catholic stands at the other end of the religious spectrum from the Theravada Buddhist. While the latter sets out in loneliness on an essentially private quest, the Catholic can always rely on others to help him on the way.

The word *catholic* means universal. In theory it is a united, as it is a world-wide, church. Its traditional structure is, however, under more fundamental strain than at any time in the past. The church is a monarchy in an age which exalts democracy; it upholds obedience in an age which worships freedom. Within the church itself papal authority is being challenged on two important points. Many priests, particularly in Holland, are demanding the right to marry and bring up children like other men. There has also been a world-wide outcry against the Pope's decision that Catholics were not permitted to use artificial methods of birth control, and there can be no doubt that his ruling is being widely ignored. Exponents of change argue that the time has come for the church to bring its organization up to date. Traditionalists reply that the structure of the church was ordered by Christ himself and cannot be changed to make it more acceptable to a permissive generation. Deep issues of principle are at stake, and it will, no doubt, be many years before the debate is resolved.

THE PROTESTANT CHURCHES

On October 31st 1517 a German friar named Martin Luther walked up to the door of Wittenburg Cathedral and nailed up a piece of paper. On it he had written down 95 points on which he took issue with a representative of the Pope who was travelling in the area at the time. Luther had no idea that his action would precipitate a major split in the Western Church. All that he intended to do was to

(opposite) *The Roman Catholic Church of the Visitation at Ein Karem, Israel, birthplace of St. John the Baptist.*

Israel Government Tourist Office

meet his opponent in a public debate. Deep issues of principle were, however, at stake. Some of the 95 points were of comparatively little importance, but there were others which challenged the very foundations of the Roman church.

Before long copies of the *95 theses* were circulating all over Germany and the friar was being held as the leader of a revolt against the power of the pope. A number of princes and nobles joined the cause. Some were genuinely convinced by Luther's arguments; others recognized an opportunity of causing trouble for the Pope and getting their hands on the wealth of the church. Encouraged by his supporters Martin Luther went on to mount ever more radical attacks on the traditional doctrines. The Emperor summoned this rebellious clergyman to appear before a meeting of all the princes of Germany and there he demanded that he stop undermining the teaching of centuries. Luther replied that he would stand by what he had written unless someone could convince him that he was wrong.

Unles I am convicted by Scripture and plain reason—I do not accept the authority of popes and councils, for they have contradicted each other—my conscience is captive to the Word of God. I cannot and I will not recant anything, for to go against conscience is neither right nor safe. God help me. Amen.

Europe was plunged into a period of religious wars which lasted off and on for more than a century.

The movement spearheaded by Martin Luther became known as the Protestant Reformation. It was *Protestant* in that it involved a protest against the established structure of the church. It was a *Reformation* in that it attempted to reform the church of abuses which had crept in over the centuries.

Luther did not only attack the pope's authority, he also challenged the right of the church as an institution to come between a Christian and his God. According to Roman doctrine, when a Christian sinned he had to go to the priest and do penance before he could receive forgiveness. Luther insisted that this was not what Jesus and the apostles had intended when they challenged men to repent. Repentance and forgiveness was a personal transaction between the sinner on the one hand and God on the other. A clergyman could *minister* to the spiritual needs of his congregation, but he could not stand between them and God. Every Christian had to be his own priest. The Protestant Churches therefore stopped calling their clergymen priests, and adopted terms like minister, pastor or presbyter (the New Testament word.)

Obviously the individual had to have some standard by which to measure his life. Luther and his followers declared that he would find it in the Bible. Throughout the previous centuries the only Bibles were in Latin and therefore could only be read by the clergy. The layman had to accept just as much as the clergyman chose to tell him about what was in it. Luther therefore settled down to the massive task of translating the whole Bible into German, while William Tyndale translated in into English and other reformers performed the task for almost every European language. They believed that they were opening up the word of God for ordinary people for 'a simple ploughboy armed with scripture was more to be trusted than all the popes and councils without it.'

Catholic critics were quick to point out a serious flaw in this argument. The Bible is a very complex document. If everyone is free to interpret it as he chooses the whole church must be plunged into chaos. The truth in this argument was demonstrated when very early Protestants began to fall out among themselves. Some, who thought that Luther had not gone far enough, tried to construct Christian communities exactly along the lines of the primitive church as described in the pages of the book of Acts. A number of enthusiasts, copying the Jerusalem Christians, sold all their possessions and tried to live a communal life. The more conventional Protestants perse-cuted these extremists in the same way that they were themselves persecuted by the Catholics.

The division of the Western Church at the Reformation

can be likened to a plate being dropped on the floor. Rather more than half the plate stayed in one piece, but the portion that broke off shattered into fragments. It would take us beyond the scope of this book to examine the varying emphases of the different Protestant churches. On the one side the Church of England preserved many of the customs and ceremonies of the medieval church, and many Anglicans would claim that their church should rightly be described as Catholic rather than Protestant. At the other extreme, the members of the Society of Friends, or Quakers, have done away with the traditional ministry, sacraments and liturgy of the church altogether, and are content to sit together in silence waiting for the Holy Spirit to move in their hearts. Today there is a strong movement for the Protestant churches to come together, and, indeed, to reopen conversations with the Eastern Orthodox and Roman Catholic churches.

For more than a century Protestant theologians have been in the forefront of the movement to submit the text of the Bible to the strictest possible examination, and many have been accused of undermining the faith of simple folk. Protestantism has always been strongest in the advanced industrial nations of Western Europe and North America. This branch of the church has therefore felt the first impact of the pressures of the modern sceptical and permissive societies. Church attendance has therefore tended to fall away more noticeably in the 20th Century in Protestant than in Catholic or Orthodox countries.

A great many vigorous Protestant communities, each in their own ways, however, continue to lead their members towards that direct confrontation with God for which Luther challenged the authorities of the church of his day. The protestant churches try to stress those doctrines which they consider central to the message of the New Testament. Some have tended towards an emotional religion of personal conversion; others have laid more stress on the dignity and order of worship. The first of these can be found in a Billy Graham revivalist meeting; the second in the presbyterian parish churches of Scotland. But whatever the particular outlook of any Protestant group may be, it is generally true that more emphasis is laid on the spiritual welfare of the individual Christian than on the structure of the church to which he belongs.

In his great classic of Protestantism John Bunyan created a parable of individual Christian's search for God. The Pilgrim's Progress took him through a world beset by all kinds of snares and temptations. On the way he had the companionship of others, bound on a similar journey, yet Christian's pilgrimage was essentially a lonely one. When he rejoices because he has arrived at his goal he speaks just of himself and the Lord that he will meet.

I see myself now at the end of my Journey, my toilsome days are ended. I am now going to see that Head that was Crowned with Thorns, and that Face that was spit upon, for me. I have formerly lived by Hear-say and Faith, but now I go where I shall live by sight, and shall be with Him, in whose Company I delight my self.

CHRISTIANITY TODAY

Although Jesus was a Semite who never left the small area of his Asian homeland, in the course of the centuries Christianity became first and foremost a European faith. The main theme of the past five centuries of history has been the compelling outward thrust of Western European civilization. The Western church—both in its Catholic and Protestant forms—took a full part in this expansion, and churches on the western pattern have been established in many parts of the world.

We therefore find the contradictory fact that today this Asian religion is regarded with suspicion in many parts of the world because of its connection with European colonialism. In almost every rebellion against western power, from the Boxer uprising in China to the Mau Mau conspiracy in Kenya, native Christian converts have been persecuted as traitors to their own people. In recent years

Christians have been stressing the fact that Jesus was not a 'white man' and that European dominance of the church must end, but it is proving hard to break the assumptions of many centuries. Western civilization is passing through a period of crisis, and the religion which has for so long underpinned that civilization is bound to be affected by the tension.

Jesus himself did not put forward a systematic body of doctrine which his followers had to accept, although on some points he was certainly more specific than the Buddha. From Paul onwards, however, Christian thinkers have put the Christian faith into systematic form. There seems to be something about the European mind which likes to get everything nicely cut and dried. Over the centuries the faith has therefore been boiled down into creeds, catechisms and all kinds of formulae. Christianity is, therefore, a very specific faith. As a result in the 17th Century Galileo could create a scandal by proclaiming that the earth was not the centre of the universe. Over two hundred years later Darwin could arouse the fury of many churchmen by showing that man had evolved from the animals. In each case an established doctrine of the church appeared to be at stake.

It has not been altogether easy for Christianity to come to terms with the new body of scientific knowledge, and a 19th Century pope was led to proclaim:

It is a mistake to teach that the Roman pontiff can or ought to reconcile himself to or agree with progress, liberalism and modern civilization.

Only a very few Christians would try to escape from the realities of life in this way. But at the same time a very real problem does remain, for Christians of all kinds have to ask themselves just how much of that very specific body of doctrine is essential to their faith. Some 'modernists' have been prepared to assert, for instance, that it does not

opposite) *Interior of Lady Huntingdon's Free Church, Worcester*

matter whether the Resurrection of Christ actually happened or not. Others cling on to the whole traditional
structure of the faith.

Christians who do not spend their time puzzling over
deep problems of theology are prepared to say that it does
not matter much what an individual believes. But over two
thousand years it has mattered very much. People have
been tortured and burnt to death because of their views on
the Trinity or the Eucharist. It is hard, therefore, to say
that these things are unimportant. But the theological
arguments of past centuries can sound singularly hollow to
modern ears.

Many have tried to cut through all the argument and
return to 'the simple teaching of Jesus', only to find that
his teaching is not as simple as would appear at first sight.
There are few, be they Christians or non Christians, who
would deny that his message of love must be preserved for
humanity. The problem for the church is to decide how far
it can 'interpret' that message for the benefit of 20th
Century man without compromising on essentials. The
Christian church as a whole is very far from reaching a
common mind on that fundamental problem.

7
Servants of the One God
ISLAM

The book of Genesis tells how for many years Abraham's wife, Sarah, failed to bear him a son. Following the custom of his people he therefore took his wife's handmaid, Hagar, and in due course she presented him with a boy called Ishmael. Shortly afterwards, however, the elderly Sarah managed to produce the infant Isaac, and in her jealousy she drove out the handmaid and her child.

This story illustrates the division which took place at an early date within the Semitic tribes. Isaac's son, Jacob was the father of the Jews who turned north into the fertile crescent, and finally fought their way to the sea. Ismael was carried by his mother into the desert country of the Arabian peninsula, where he became the ancestor of the Arab people.

Arabia in the time of Mohammed

Today the Arabian peninsula is one of the least hospitable places on earth. The sun beats down with vicious intensity on mile after mile of parched desert. Bedouin tribes manage to survive in this empty land, though they have to be prepared to fight their neighbours at any time to preserve their rights over the water holes which provide a slender life-line for themselves and their animals. The way of life of these nomadic tribesmen has changed little over the 1,400 years which have passed since the prophet Mohammed was born.

It is probable that in those days the land was rather more fertile than it is today. The centre of the peninsula, then as now, was taken up by the vast desert of the Empty Quarter, but there are signs that more land was fit for cultivation along the coastal strip. Despite this, agriculture always brought a poor return for labour, and Mohammed's countrymen gathered their wealth by the traditional methods of trading and raiding.

Products of Arabia were exported for sale in the more heavily populated areas to the north and the east. Incense, sweet smelling woods, myrrh, resin and dates were all sought after in the markets of Constantinople and India. Arabia was set across one of the main arteries of the world's trade. Caravans laden with spices and fine fabrics of the east followed the trade routes which passed through the flourishing town of Mecca where the prophet was born.

Naturally these caravans had to be guarded against the tribes which would swoop out of the desert when they were least expected. The capture of a rich caravan would be a great event for Bedouins who could barely manage to keep themselves alive. Such successes, however, were rare, and for the rest of the time these fierce warriors had to content themselves with stealing cattle from their neighbours. Warfare was therefore an integral part of the way of life of the tribes. The only justice was the harsh law of the vendetta. Since all strangers were enemies, it was essential that every man should be able to trust the brother of his own tribe.

Each tribe looked to its gods to give it victory in battle. If one god failed to deliver what was expected of him then he would be rejected for another. The citizens of Mecca managed to exploit the religious beliefs of their countrymen to their own profit. Every year thousands of pilgrims poured into the city to worship at the Ka'ba, which was the most famous shrine in the whole peninsula. This was the centre of the cult of three goddesses. The most important member of this trio was al'Uzzah, the mighty one, who was the special protectress of the inhabitants of the city.

Along the trade routes there could also be found small pockets of Jews and Christians. The former were traders, who controlled a great deal of the wealth of the land. They were therefore the object of considerable envy and even hatred. The Christians, probably humbler folk, belonged to branches of the church which had been denounced as 'unorthodox'. Many had suffered bitter persecution from their fellow Christians before seeking refuge in Arabia.

THE LIFE OF MOHAMMED

Our information about the lives of the Buddha and Jesus is drawn from narratives which were written down some time after their deaths. When we study Mohammed, however, we can base our knowledge on sources dating from his own lifetime. Despite this, it remains difficult to sort out reliable fact from later additions. Mohammed's own sayings, which make up the Koran, tell us comparatively little about his life. Many traditions have been handed down, and Muslim scholars have spent an immense amount of effort trying to distinguish those which are reliable from those which are not. Much of the· *hadith*, or accepted tradition, is no doubt true, but, as with the Buddha and Jesus, it is hard to make statements with any certainty. Whatever their historical accuracy, however, these stories are important because they have become an essential part of the Moslem inheritance.

The Prophet was born in about 570 A.D. His father, a respected member of one of the Meccan tribes, died before his son was born. It was common practice at the time for wealthy wives, who did not want the bother of bringing up their own children, to give their new born babies to the care of tribeswomen, who took them back to their villages and acted as foster mothers during the early years of the child's life. In the year that Mohammed was born the women came as usual to pick up their charges. Being a widow, the prophet's mother was too poor to engage the services of a healthy woman. When all the other babies had been disposed of, there was just one tribeswoman left to take the infant. Halima had arrived last in Mecca because her camel was worn out. She was also so undernourished that her breasts were dry, but tradition reports that the moment she picked up the widow's child they filled with milk. As with the Buddha and Jesus such stories are designed to show that the young Mohammed was no ordinary child. It is recorded that Jewish and Christian holy men came from miles around to study the oval white birth mark, which was supposed to be the sign of a prophet. In course of time Halima, the foster mother, became so frightened by these signs that she returned the child to his natural mother.

When Mohammed was six his mother died, and thereafter he was brought up by his grandfather. When he was old enough he began to travel the caravan routes, looking after his family's business interests. During this period of his life he learnt to be a warrior, ever on his guard against the surprise attacks of raiders. He became renowned for his competence, and gained the nick-name of al—Arun, the loyal one.

In course of time he became camel master for a widow called Khadya who was fifteen years his senior. When he was 25 he married his employer. Khadija was able to give him the status and wealth which he had lacked as an orphan child, but she gave him much more as well. A wise woman of even temper, she was able to support her husband through the great spiritual crises which were to follow. Although Mohammed had other, younger wives, Khadija always held the highest place in his affections.

Mohammed is the only one of the three great religious leaders of whom we have any information about physical appearance. He was, it is reported, a powerfully built man of medium height with a large head and high, broad forehead. He had a full beard and head of jet black hair which later turned grey. Deep black, piercing eyes, a hooked Semitic nose and large mouth combined to make up a striking face. He had a charming smile, but, when a vein stood out on his temple, men learnt to fear his fierce anger.

The Call
While travelling the trade routes he would have the opportunity of talking with Christians and Jews. Although

it does not appear that he ever learnt much about these two Semitic religions, it was almost certainly from them that he picked up the basic idea of monotheism—that God is one. As the years passed he became more and more taken up with the quest for true religion, and he spent much of his time meditating on Mount Hira.

One night, when alone on the slopes of the mountain, Mohammed had a vision. In it the angel Gabriel came to him with a piece of silk on which some words were written. 'Recite', said the angel. 'What shall I recite?' asked Mohammed. The angel did not reply, but repeated his demand again and yet again. Mohammed felt as though he was going to choke to death. 'What then shall I recite?' he asked a third time in desperation. This time the angel answered.

Recite in the name of thy Lord who created man from blood coagulated. Recite! Thy Lord is wondrous kind who by the pen has taught mankind things which they knew not, being blind.

The tradition tells how he awoke in a state of terror.

It was as though the words were written on my heart. So I went forth and then when I was midway on the mountain I heard a voice from heaven saying, 'O Mohammed, Thou are the prophet of God and I am Gabriel. I raised my head towards the heaven to see who was speaking, and lo, Gabriel in the form of a man with feet astride the horizon. I stood gazing at him, moving neither forward nor backward; then I began to turn my face away from him but, towards whatever region of the sky I looked, I saw him as before.

Overwhelmed by this experience, Mohammed rushed back home to find peace in Khadija's arms.

In the period which followed the vision Mohammed experienced what men have called 'the dark night of the soul'. He was terrified that his fellow townsmen would turn against him if they discovered what had happened; he also began to fear that he had been deserted by God, and even contemplated suicide. Then on the night which Moslems call the Night of Destiny the voice of Gabriel came back to him, reassuring him that he was indeed the

Lord's chosen prophet. He was instructed to go out and preach what he had learnt.

The Hejira

From this time onwards Mohammed began to build up a little group of *companions*, who accepted his message that God was one. The first convert to this new faith was probably the prophet's close friend Abu Bakr. Later six travellers from the inland town of Medina listened to his teaching, and returned home to establish a community of believers in their home town.

Mohammed had been afraid that his preaching would arouse opposition, and these fears proved well founded. At first the Meccans did not take much notice of the little community, gathered round its prophet. After a time, however, they began to realize that Mohammed's message posed a serious threat to their city's life. In the first place he was saying that their gods were false. They might have been prepared to let him attack some of the less important gods but they were bitterly offended when he denounced al'Ussah and her sister goddesses. No doubt many of the Meccans were genuinely devoted to the worship of these deities, and feared that they would bring evil on the city if the people turned away from worshipping them. More mundane issues were, however, also at stake. The citizens drew a great deal of wealth from the travellers who came on the annual pilgrimage to the Ka'ba. By attacking their gods, the prophet was threatening their very livelihood.

Mohammed would probably have been killed at that early stage had he not been protected by the traditional family solidarity. Even those members of his tribe who did not accept his message were committed to protecting the life of their brother. Members of the young community who could not command such protection, however, often had to suffer for their beliefs. The prophet therefore advised them to take any opportunity that offered to slip away and find refuge with their fellow Moslems at Medina.

At last in the year 622 the Meccans settled on a plan to assassinate Mohammed. No one family was prepared to carry the blame for the act, so all ten of the tribes of Mecca agreed to contribute men to a band which would carry out the deed. But, just as the assassins were gathering round his house, Mohammed managed to slip away with his friend Abu Bakr. They had to hide in a cave while their enemies searched the countryside for them. Tradition says that a spider spun its web and two pigeons built a nest in the mouth of the cave to deceive the pursuers into thinking that nobody had entered it.

On the 20th September 622 Mohammed finally joined his friends at Medina. The flight from Mecca, known as the *Hejira*, marks the beginning of the Moslem calendar. The place where he alighted from his camel was set aside as the first *mosque* of the Moslem world.

The Struggle for Power

Once established in Medina, Mohammed continued to live a simple and unpretentious life, sweeping the floor of his own house and lighting his own fire. But he was no longer just a preacher with a message about God; he had become the leader of a powerful political force. The strength of his Moslems lay in the fact that for the first time a group had emerged with loyalties larger than those of mere blood relationship. It was unheard of that Medinans and Meccans should fight as a single unit, and only a man of the most powerful personality could have held such a group together.

The prophet was a man of war. This may seem surprising to people brought up within other creeds, but in the Arabian peninsula at that time every man had to be a warrior. Even more surprising perhaps, is the fact that when occasion demanded he was prepared to break solemn agreements, arrange political assassinations and even engage in the traditional pastime of raiding unwary settlements and caravans. Again, this was the accepted behaviour of his time and none of Mohammed's enemies ever accused him of being morally wicked on account of the methods that he used in his struggle against the unbelievers.

Within the lifetime of the prophet the new faith spread across the Arabian peninsula. After a series of sharp battles the Meccans were forced to allow the exile to return at the head of 10,000 followers. When he was inside the city he climbed onto the Ka'ba shrine and proclaimed his message of the one God. At first the Meccans expected the three goddesses, whose shrines had been defiled, to demonstrate their anger, but, when no disasters occurred, these old enemies began to accept his message.

Mohammed's last Pilgrimage

Cynics have remarked that by the time the Meccans joined the forces of Islam, it had become clear that they would be able to make a good thing out of it. Mohammed had broken the Jewish control of the Arabian trade routes, and—what was enough to gladden the heart of any of the city's traders—pilgrims kept on coming to the ancient shrines, although now they worshipped the one God instead of al'Uzzah and her sisters.

Mohammed continued to live in his simple house in Medina. In 632, the last year of his life, he set out on a final pilgrimage to the holy shrines in the city of his birth. As he travelled along the way 80,000 of the faithful joined in his train. At the appointed places along the route he performed traditional ceremonies which had been observed by heathen pilgrims for centuries before he was born. When he arrived in the city the word of the Lord came on him, and he spoke with the true voice of prophecy once again.

After the pilgrimage he returned to Medina, and died on the 7th June 632—the 11th year of the Moslem era. Tradition says that the angel of death came and asked permission to take him away, and the prophet instructed the angel to carry out its orders. He was buried in his own house, where his tomb still stands.

When Abu Bakr heard the news he spoke to all the people. 'If anyone worships Mohammed, Mohammed is dead. If anyone worships God, God is alive, immortal'. The prophet had lived and died an uncompromising mono

The Prophet's Mosque at Medina

theist. There was only one God, and no man could compete with him. Mohammed was a prophet and a servant of God in the line of prophets from Abraham and Moses.

THE KORAN

Every major religion has its sacred writings. Beside the hundreds of volumes which form the canon of Mahayana Buddhism, the Koran is a comparatively slender work, yet Moslems hold it more sacred than even the most conventional of Christians would his Bible. To them it is the word of God, dictated through the mouth of the prophet.

The traditions describe how Mohammed's body became rigid and excessively heavy when the spirit of prophesy came upon him. On one occasion it happened when he was riding a camel, and onlookers could see the creature bend and nearly fall under the unaccustomed weight. On another occasion Mohammed was sitting with his foot on a friend's knee. Suddenly the Prophet stiffened and the weight of his limb almost broke his companion's leg.

According to tradition Mohammed himself was illiterate. As soon as he spoke the words of prophesy they were committed to memory by his followers. At some later date they were set down in a form which has been accepted as being the most perfect Arabic ever written. Since the word of God came to Mohammed in Arabic, Moslems insist that the Koran cannot be translated into other languages. It is important, therefore, that every Moslem should learn Arabic. Those that cannot achieve this commit the verses of the Koran to memory parrot fashion, for it is considered more important that they should *possess* the sacred word of God than they should *understand* what it means.

As a book the Koran has to be treated with the greatest respect. It may not be placed under any other volume and no one may talk while it is being read. Indeed it is thought

Procession on the eve of the feast of Mouloud

to possess almost magical qualities. Verses sewn up in leather can be worn as charms against sickness, death in battle or almost any other misfortune.

THE NATURE OF GOD

The Koran proclaims that God is one. Mohammed used the name *Allah*, which came from the old Semitic syllable Il, meaning God. Before his time Allah was just one among the many gods of Arabia. The prophet claimed that all the other gods were false.

Both Jews and Christians talk of God as being *omnipotent*—all powerful. Yet it is in the doctrines of Islam that this idea is carried relentlessly through to its logical conclusion. The words of the Koran are written on many Moslem tombstones.

Allah: there is no god but Him, the Living, the Eternal One. Neither slumber nor sleep overtakes Him. He is what the heavens and the earth contain. Who can intercede with Him except by His permission? He knows what is before and behind men. They can grasp only that part of his knowledge that He wills. His throne is as vast as the heavens and the earth, and the preservation of both does not weary Him. He is the Exalted, the Immense One.

An omnipotent God must have absolute power over the lives of men, and Moslems look on the future as being in the hands of God in a way that even Christians and Jews do not. No Moslem would say 'I shall do such-and-such a thing tomorrow', without adding, 'If Allah wills it.' At parting one Moslem will say, 'Until tomorrow,' to which his friend must reply 'May Allah bring us there'. These are not empty forms of words. It is blasphemy for a believer to claim that he can foresee the events of the next day. It has been pointed out that this fatalistic outlook tends to sap initiative. When a Moslem meets suffering, either in his own life or in the lives of others, he is very inclined to shrug and say that it is the will of Allah. He therefore has little incentive to change the circumstances which create the suffering.

Allah is all powerful; man is weak and helpless by comparison. The duty of the believer is to surrender himself completely. The very word *Islam* means surrender. Beside Allah man is as nothing.

Allah is the light of the heavens and the earth. His light may be compared to a niche that enshrines a lamp, the lamp within a crystal of star-like brilliance. It is lit from a blessed olive tree neither eastern nor western. Its very oil would almost shine forth, though no fire touch it. Light upon light; Allah guides to His light whom He will .

To Allah belongs what the heavens and the earth contain. He has knowledge of all your thoughts and actions. On the day when they return to Him He will declare to them all that they have done. He has knowledge of all things.

If God is all-powerful it is clearly futile for a man to rebel against his own destiny. The point is made in a story told by an Islamic poet.

A man once went to visit mighty King Solomon and found the Angel of Death present there. Believing that the latter looked at him angrily he asked King Solomon the favour of being instantly removed to far-distant India by the winds at the King's command. The King fulfilled his wish and then questioned the Angel of Death, who replied. 'I was watching this man not with anger but with astonishment, because the Lord has commanded me to kill him today in India. Seeing him here I was wondering how God could have been mistaken.' Thus I have learnt never to doubt the Lord, his ways and his orders.

THE JUDGEMENT

The dominant theme in the Koran is the coming judgement of God. We have seen (page 73) that the other Semitic religions share the belief that men will be called upon to face the judgement of a righteous God, who will assign some to bliss and others to misery.

The Koran paints the coming day of judgement in the most vivid colours. The first trumpet will be blown, at which all men will fall to the ground. The second trumpet will be blown and the dead will rise from their graves. To them it will seem as if no time at all had passed since the moment that they died. Then the heavens will be rolled back like a scroll, and the throne of Allah will appear, borne by eight angels, with the heavenly host drawn up in columns on either side. When all is ready the humans will be brought for judgement before the throne. Every man will find that the record of his life is written in the Book of Deeds.

On one side of the throne will be set the true believers who are destined for the joys of Paradise. They can look forward to an endless existence of bliss when all their wants are catered for. They will find food in plenty as well as 'virgins as fair as corals and rubies'.

Reclining there upon soft couches, they shall feel neither the scorching heat nor the biting cold. Trees will spread their shade around them, and fruits will hang in clusters over them.   They shall be served with silver dishes, and beakers as large as goblets; silver goblets which they themselves shall measure: and cups brim-full with ginger-flavoured water from the Fount of Selsabil. They shall be attended by boys graced with eternal youth, who to the beholder's eyes will seem like sprinkled pearls. When you gaze upon that scene you will behold a kingdom blissful and glorious.

When unbelievers come face to face with their judge, they will find that it is too late for repentance.

Woe on that day to the disbelievers! Begone to that Hell which you deny! Depart into the shadow that will rise high in three columns, giving neither shade nor shelter from the flames and throwing up sparks as huge as towers, as bright as yellow camels!   Woe on that day to the disbelievers! On that day they shall not speak, nor shall their pleas be accepted.

There is one serious objection to this simple view of judgement according to the works of men. If Allah is in truth all-knowing and all-powerful then he must know beforehand—and indeed ordain beforehand—which men shall be saved and which shall be damned. This doctrine, known as *predestination*, has also been held by some Christians. On the face of it, it appears monstrously unjust. How could men be blamed for living according to a destiny which was settled before they were ever born? But Mohammed, with his overriding concern for the omnipotence of God, does not shrink from such a conclusion. The Koran assumes that the fate of all men is sealed, and yet they must still be held responsible for their own actions.

THE FIVE PILLARS OF ISLAM

The prophet laid five duties on his followers. In all parts of the Moslem world a man's claim to be a true believer is assessed by his diligence in carrying out these obligations.

(opposite) *Al Azhar Mosque, Cairo*

U.A.R. Tourist and Information Centre

The Confession

'There is no God but Allah and Mohammed is his prophet'. These are the words of confession of the Moslem faith. Once a man has made this simple declaration in the presence of witnesses he can account himself a believer. This form of words is much simpler than any creed devised by the Christian church, yet in a real sense it contains the whole of the Muslim faith. It has been one of the great strengths of Islam that it is the easiest to understand of all the world's great religions.

Prayer

Visitors to Moslem countries cannot fail to be impressed at the way in which people stop whatever they may be doing five times every day to say their prayers. Those who live in the towns can carry on their business until they hear the *muezzin* calling the faithful to worship from the minaret on the mosque. He repeats each statement at least once.

God is most great.
I testify that there is no God but Allah.
I testify that Mohammed is God's prophet.
Come to prayer, come to security.
God is most great.

Travellers through the open countryside have to watch the sun as it climbs across the sky so that they can judge the proper time for prayer.

At sunset, last thing at night, at dawn, at noon and in the afternoon all Muslims kneel down with their faces towards Mecca. They perform the ceremonial prostrations as they repeat the traditional words of worship.

Mohammed put aside one day when the faithful should gather together for communal prayer. Perhaps to show that he was independent both of Judaism and Christianity, he set it on Friday. This is not, however, a Sabbath of the Jewish type, for no restrictions are placed on work. At midday all the men gather at the mosque to say their prayers together. Since Allah dwells everywhere, the mosque is just a meeting place for the faithful and not a place sacred in itself. An *imam* (teacher) stands at the front and the whole congregation follows him as exactly as possible so that all move and chant in perfect unison.

Praise belongs to God, Lord of the Worlds,
The Compassionate, the Merciful,
King of the Day of Judgement,
It is Thee we worship and Thee we ask for help.
Guide us on the straight path,
The path of those whom thou hast favoured,
Not the path of those who incur Thine anger nor of
those who go astray.

To the Moslem prayer is a duty, and he does not expend his energies worrying about what he gets out of it. It is not a means of pleading with God, but simply the method by which God's creatures give him the honour that is rightly his.

Almsgiving

The Koran instructs the faithful to give alms regularly to the poor. What will surprise the Christian is that the Moslem is expected to give alms, not for the sake of the poor who are in need, but in order to improve his own chances of achieving a place in heaven. This is made clear in the Koran.

We have bestowed the Book on those of our Servants whom We have chosen. Some of them sin against their souls, some follow a middle course, and some, by Allah's leave, vie with each other in charitable works:
This is the supreme virtue.
   They shall enter the gardens of Eden, where they shall be decked with pearls and bracelets of gold, and arrayed in robes of silk.

It is an unhappy result of this emphasis on almsgiving that Moslem countries never seem to lack for beggars. Every Friday they can be seen gathered round the door of the mosque looking for the gifts which worshippers will hand out before going to worship.

Fasting

Each year the whole of the month of Ramadan is set

aside as a great fast. Between dawn and dusk the faithful take no food or drink, and many will not even swallow their own spittle. The Moslem year consists of twelve lunar months, and so Ramadan does not always fall at the same season. When it comes in the hottest time the fast can cause considerable hardship. Since there are no limitations to the amount eaten and drunk in the hours when the sun is down, it does not, however, constitute a hazard to health.

The Hajj

The last of the pillars of Islam is the *hajj,* or pilgrimage to Mecca, which every Moslem is expected to make at least once in his lifetime if it is possible for him to do so. In Mohammed's time all Moslems lived reasonably close to

Pilgrims arriving by plane for the Hajj

the holy city, but today over a million pilgrims arrive in Mecca, some of whom have travelled from places as far off as Indonesia and South America. Many travel in specially chartered planes, ships and trains. Others undertake immense overland journeys, sometimes taking them a year or more. Settlements of West African Moslems can be found in the Sudan consisting of men who have set out to walk across the continent, and never returned to their homes.

The pilgrims walk the last miles to the city with heads shaved and wearing two seamless white sheets. When they enter the sacred enclosure they walk seven times around the Ka'ba, which now stands draped in black, while imams lead them in prayer. The practice of making such magic circles is often found in animist cults and this ritual must date back before the prophet. British children weave similar pagan charms when they dance round the mulberry bush.

Pilgrims at the Prophet's Mosque in Mecca are gathered round the Ka'ba– Islam's holiest shrine

Not every Moslem can perform the pilgrimage, but a remarkable number do. Thereafter they have the right to call themselves *Hajj*. This is a distinction to be carried with great pride.

THE JIHAD

Mohammed taught that believers should not hesitate to use the sword in the cause of the true faith. In his view death was a trivial thing compared to unbelief. The Koran urges the faithful to go to war in the name of the one God.

Proclaim a woeful punishment to the unbelievers, except those idolaters who have honoured their treaties with you and aided none against you. With these keep faith, until their treaties have run their term. Allah loves the righteous.

When the sacred months are over slay the idolaters wherever you find them. Arrest them, besiege them, and lie in ambush everywhere for them. If they repent and take to prayer and pay the alms-tax, let them go their way. Allah is forgiving and merciful.

No mercy was to be shown to idolaters and polytheists. Mohammed did, however, give instructions that Christians and Jews should be treated with respect, for they were 'People of the Book', who had travelled some distance towards the truth.

After the prophet died his followers obeyed his instructions and carried a holy war across the lands of the Middle East. The Persian Empire, which had for centuries withstood the power of Rome, fell before the Arab armies. Before long Constantinople itself was threatened. Palestine, with its holy places of the Jewish and Christian religions, was engulfed in the forward sweep of the Islamic Empire.

The Moslem armies were not nearly as bloodthirsty as their official creed might lead one to expect. In many places they were welcomed by the conquered people because they offered a milder and more just form of government than that which they replaced. The Peoples of

the Book were allowed to continue with their own forms
of worship, provided they paid a special poll tax.

THE ISLAMIC EMPIRE

For many centuries the Moslems had a civilization which
put that of Western Europe to shame. In the middle of the
10th Century the Spanish town of Cordoba could boast of
700 mosques, 300 public baths, and 70 libraries which
between them possessed no less than 1,400,000 volumes.
Science and scholarship flourished, and the Arabs were
responsible for introducing the Indian numeral system to
Europe. In the course of time, however, this great empire
found itself caught between the pressure of Christian
Europeans in the West and heathen Turks in the East. The
libraries were burnt and many of the great monuments of
the civilization were destroyed.

THE SUNNA AND THE SHI'A

Like Christianity, Islam has at various times been divided
into rival factions, though divisions have never become so
deeply entrenched as those between different branches of
the Christian church. The main division in Islam is between
the factions known as the Sunna and the Shi'a.

When Mohammed died his place as *caliph* (leader) of the
Moslem world was taken by his old friend and companion
Abu Bakr. There were some, however, who thought that the
position should have gone to his cousin and son-in-law, Ali.
Two other caliphs followed Abu Bakr before at last Ali
succeeded to the title. His reign was, however, troubled
and in the end he was deposed and murdered.

Shi'a Moslems never accepted the new ruling house, and
continued to uphold the claims of the house of Ali. Soon
they developed a new doctrine, that Ali had been the Imam
of the Moslem world, and that he was succeeded in every
generation by an Imam, who was the interpreter of the

faith to his own age. Some went so far as to declare that 'whoever dies without recognizing the Imam of his time dies the death of a pagan'.

Sunna Moslems disapproved of this doctrine because they thought that it detracted from the special position of Mohammed. While the Sunnas remained unified, the Shi'as became increasingly divided into a large number of sects. But the divisions in Islam are not as deep as those in Christianity. A Moslem can travel around the world and go into any mosque. As long as he can make the profession of faith he will not be excluded. Different Christian groups, in contrast, are only just beginning to see whether it might not be possible to worship together, and at the Eucharist Orthodox, Catholic and Protestant remain divided.

THE SHARI'A

Through the centuries, Moslem society has been under-pinned by its legal system, known as the *Shari'a*. There are several codes of law in use in different parts of the Moslem world, but all work on the same underlying principle. Cases brought before the courts are decided by reference to the Koran and the traditions which are accepted as dating back to the prophet.

All actions by believers can be put into one of five categories—obligatory, recommended, indifferent, disapproved or prohibited. In the last category would fall the prohibitions on the eating of pork and the drinking of wine. In Saudi Arabia, where the strict letter of the Shari'a is still enforced, the western distinction between murder and manslaughter is not taken into account in cases of killing, and thieves are punished by having their hands cut off.

Saudi Arabian tribesmen still follow much the same kind of life as their ancestors, and it is therefore possible to enforce an unchanging code of law. In countries like Egypt and Turkey, however, life has changed so much over the centuries that the strict letter of the Shari'a has needed modification in many ways. In theory this modification is impossible; in practice, adaptation to changing circumstances is essential if society is to function at all. Some would say that the inflexibility of the Shari'a has held the Moslem countries back and prevented them from fulfilling their potential in the modern world.

THE PLACE OF WOMEN

In the Arabian society of Mohammed's time, women were treated as creatures without rights. The prophet gave several instructions which were designed to improve their position. A man could have only four wives, and he was not allowed that many unless he could keep each of them in a fitting manner. As we have seen, Mohammed was himself a devoted lover and husband. Yet his outlook on the status of women remained that of a man of his times. 'Women are your tillage,' states the Koran. In accounts of the joys of heaven they only appear as loving companions for men.

The Koran gives instructions to women to behave at all times with proper modesty.

Enjoin believing women to turn their eyes away from temptation and to preserve their chastity; to cover their adornments (except such as are normally displayed); to draw their veils over their bosoms and not to reveal their finery except to their husbands, their fathers, their husbands' fathers, their sons, their step-sons, their brothers, their brothers' sons, their sisters' sons, their women-servants, and their slave-girls; male attendants lacking in natural vigour, and children who have no carnal knowledge of women. And let them not stamp their feet in walking so as to reveal their hidden trinkets.

Over the centuries this has been interpreted as sanctioning the practice of *purdah*, whereby, once a woman was married she remained shut up in her husband's compound. If she was allowed to go out at all she went veiled from head to foot.

In Buddhist Ceylon, Hindu India and Jewish Israel, women have already held the position of prime minister.

No Christian country has as yet elevated a woman to that state, but western women have improved their position greatly during the 20th Century. A revolution is also taking place in the Moslem world. In some of the more advanced nations women can record their vote, though there is still no sign of them taking a leading part in politics. But the old traditions die hard. The divorce laws of some Moslem countries still appear very unjust to western eyes, and the system of purdah continues to flourish, particularly among the higher classes, in some of the more traditional Moslem nations.

ISLAM TODAY

The need to adapt the Shari'a and the pressure for the abolition of customs like purdah illustrate the problems which face conventional Islam in the modern world. The rising generation is not prepared to accept that everything new must be judged by the standards of the past, or that backwardness and poverty come from the will of Allah rather than the laziness and self-seeking of men. There is no doubt that Islam, like Christianity, faces a period of reappraisal, during which it must disentangle that part of its creed which must remain unchanging from that part which can be adapted to meet the demands of a new age. The emphasis on the absolute authority of the Koran and the unchanging nature of tradition makes this a very difficult process.

It would not be right, however, to give the impression that Islam is more beset with problems than other religions. It has great strengths which are helping it to expand in many parts of the world at a time when other faiths are contracting. The Prophet taught the brotherhood of all believers, and Moslems take little account of a man's race or colour, as long as he is prepared to make the confession of faith. When the Arabian empire was first expanding, European soldiers were astonished to discover that its armies were commanded by a negro general. In very recent times black power leaders in America have professed at least a nominal conversion to this faith which is not tainted with doctrines of European supremacy.

Christian clergy often remind their congregations that theirs is a missionary gospel, and that every church member should go out to convert others. Generally their words pass unheeded. To Moslems such an idea would seem so obvious as not to need repeating. There have never been any missionary societies within Islam, but merchants have taken their simple faith in one God with them as they travelled the trade routes of the world.

The strong and totally unsentimental message of Islam does appeal to some deep need in man's make-up. Once an individual has made the confession that there is no God but Allah and Mohammed is his prophet, he belongs to a great brotherhood. This gives him confidence to look any man in the eye with pride. The Moslem has no need to copy the habits or customs of others, for he is assured that he is one of the elect of Allah. He can live his life boldly, content that, whatever the next day may bring, it is in the hands of the all-powerful and all-knowing God.

8
The Religions Meet One Another

The peoples of the world are in a constant state of movement. The process of trade, settlement and warfare carry men and ideas away from the homes in which they were born and deposit them in other parts of the globe. It is necessary to study the world's religions in isolation from each other, but, of course, they have not stayed separate throughout the course of history. Sometimes when they have met, the one has simply tried to overcome the other. We will not try to trace the course of this rivalry, but will look briefly at those occasions when the meeting of the great religions has produced something distinctively new. This process has mainly taken place in the lands where civilization was born, between the Fertile Crescent in the west and the river valleys of India in the east.

THE SUFIS

We have seen that the doctrines of Islam very quickly swept across the Persian Empire. As long as men relied mainly on land routes for communication, this could be called the cross-roads of the world. Persians had long been in touch with Hindus and Buddhists from the East and Christians and Jews from the West. They also had an ancient religion of their own, called Zoroastrianism, which today only survives in the tiny Parsee community in India. Within a comparatively short time a school of Moslems, called Sufis, began to draw its inspiration from all these many sources, as well as the religion of the Prophet.

Like the Hindus, the Sufis sought to find a deep union between man and God. They were able to quote texts

Three religious cultures meet in Delhi

from the Koran to justify their quest. 'Wherever you turn, there is the face of God,' states one verse. Another goes so far as to say that God is nearer to man than the veins of his neck. Instead of concentrating on the omnipotence of Allah, they began to speak of his love for man in terms which were drawn from Christianity.

Up to this point the Sufis had been changing the emphasis of Islam, but they had not contradicted official teaching. But then some of them began to teach doctrines which seemed to strike at the very foundation of the faith. It is impossible, declared one, to say that there is a difference between 'I' and 'God' for this is to deny the unity of Allah. A 10th Century Sufi teacher went so far as to declare 'I am truth',

I am he whom I love, and he whom I love is I,
We are two spirits dwelling in one body.
If thou seest me, thou seest him,
If thou seest him, thou seest us both.

Such sentiments may be Hinduism, and they may be

Buddhism; they most certainly are not Islam. The teacher was therefore crucified as a heretic. After that Sufis were careful not to use such language, but they continue to seek that mystical union between God and the soul, which is looked upon with suspicion by orthodox Moslems.

In the freer atmosphere of the modern world some Sufis would go so far as to deny that they are Moslems and would rather stress their links with the East and with Zoroastrianism. Many of them have a gentleness and a sense of unity with creatures of all kinds which is more characteristic of Hinduism and Buddhism than with Islam. But there are many kinds of Sufism. In North Africa and elsewhere in the Moslem world there flourish a number of Sufi *dervish* sects. Some observers have described how some dervishes work themselves into a frenzy in which they can slash themselves with knives without feeling any pain, but not all of the sects indulge in such extreme practices.

SIKHISM

In the Middle Ages the Moslems began to conquer India. According to the Koran the Hindus who lived in the sub-continent were idolaters, and so deserved no mercy. In practice the invaders made no attempt to kill off the whole population. There was, however, continued conflict between the followers of the two religions, which has tragically continued down to our own times.

One Emperor of India, the great Akbar, decided that the only way to end bloodshed and rivalry among his people was to establish a religion which combined the best features of all religions. He therefore declared that his people should not think of themselves as Hindus or Moslems, but as believers in one God. Akbar's experiment failed, and his successors returned to the orthodox Islam of their ancestors.

The Emperor was not the only person, however, who recognized the evils of having two warring faiths in the one land. Half a century earlier a Muslem rug weaver named Kabir, who lived in the city of Benares, had taught the same message. His words were heard by a Hindu called Nanah, who is looked upon as the founder of the Sikh religion.

When Nanah was about 36 years old he had a vision of heaven in which Brahma appeared and offered him a drink of nectar. From that time onward he travelled the length of India preaching his new doctrine, 'There is no Hindu and no Moslem'.

The Sikh religion combined elements of both faiths. From Hinduism Nanah preserved the idea of the wheel of rebirth and the spiritual exercises of devotion to God. The end of man's striving remained the 'blowing out' of nirvana, rather than the last day of judgement. From Islam he drew an emphatic monotheism. God, who he named Hari, was one and all powerful. Men had to submit themselves to the will of Hari absolutely, and they suffered when they rebelled against him. He also provided his followers with a sacred book, known as the Granth.

Nanah taught his followers to lead a healthy life, abjuring drugs but eating meat. Before long the Sikhs became renowned for their physical strength. In the early days they were pacifists, but during the 17th Century they came into conflict with the Moslem rulers and turned into warriors. During this period the Sikhs followed leaders, who were known as *gurus*. The last guru, Gobind Rai, organized his followers into a brotherhood of the pure. Every Sikh was received into the fellowship by a baptism of sword and nectar. After that he had to wear the five signs of membership: trousers, a dagger, an iron bracelet, a comb and hair that was never cut. Gobind Rai also took the title Singh, the Lion, which he passed on to his followers. He was killed with all his sons in 1708. From that time the Sikhs have had no human leader but have looked upon the Granth as their spiritual guru. They have had to face many periods of persecution, but the structure which Gobind Rai gave to their religion has proved strong enough to hold them together.

THE BAHA'IS

There is a sect in Shi'a Islam which believes that there were only twelve Imams. The last of these did not die, but became invisible. In course of time he would return to lead his people once again. Many men at one time and another have claimed to be this Imam.

In 1844 a young man named Murza 'Ali Muhammed started to preach in Iraq (Persia), claiming that the time had come for the Imam to return. He took the title Bab, stating that he was not the Imam but a forerunner, like John the Baptist was the forerunner of Jesus. Bab's followers rose in rebellion against the government and Bab was executed in 1850. There followed a period of uncertainty, and two half brothers disputed the right to be called Bab's successor. The majority of the members of the sect accepted the elder of the two, who had taken the name Baha'u'llah. In 1866 Baha proclaimed that he was 'He whom God shall manifest'.

Such incidents are comparatively common in Islam, but the teaching of Baha began to diverge more and more from accepted doctrine. Before long the Baha'is were denying the authority of the Koran and the mission of Mohammed himself. Baha declared that truth does not lie in any one religion. God had sent a series of prophets into the world. Among these he included the Buddha and Zoroaster as well as Semites such as Abraham, Jesus and Mohammed. He admitted that at times they appear to disagree with each other. He explained this by saying that a teacher has always to put across his message in a way that would be understood by his pupils, according to their age and ability. Thus Mohammed had to talk to Arabians in terms of a physical heaven and hell, though they did not exist. The message of each prophet superceded that of his predecessor, but each time a prophet appeared he was always rejected by a great proportion of the people he came to teach. Jesus was rejected by the Jews, Mohammed by the Christians and he himself was rejected by the Mohammedans.

Baha's son continued his father's teaching and gave it emphasis to appeal to a world-wide audience. He declared that the Baha'i faith was opposed to all forms of division between one man and another. There should be no race, sect, class or religious prejudice, for all mankind was one and all religion was one. He even looked for a time when there would be a united world, governed by representatives of all people.

This universalist faith has gained considerable following outside of its native land. Today the government of Iraq is dominated by the Baha'ist party. It has unfortunately chosen to rule on totalitarian lines, so that, as has happened with other religions, the faith in action does not measure up to its high ideals.

9
Religion and its Critics

It would take another book to do justice to the subject of religion in the world today. In the course of dealing with the individual religions we have considered some of the reassessments which are necessary as they try to make contact with modern man. In conclusion we might note, necessarily in rather crude form, just three of the main criticisms which have been levelled against religion as a whole. It may be noted that they have all been formulated in the West and they are all more specifically directed at the Semitic than at the Eastern forms of faith.

THE MARXIST CRITICISM

The founder of communism came from a German Jewish family and early became involved in the revolutionary struggles of 19th Century Europe. In course of time he began to work out a theory of history which could be applied to all periods of man's development. In it he refused to give any weight to motives which might be called spiritual, and said that man was an economic animal, whose overriding aim was to improve his material wealth, if necessary at the expense of others.

Within this broad framework, Marx branded religion as 'the opiate of the proletariat'. By that he meant that it was a drug offered to the poor to induce them to forget injustice and the misery of their lives. Ruling classes, who wanted to keep the earth's wealth to themselves could very cheaply offer rewards to the masses in a future life if they accepted their lot dutifully and obediently in this life.

THE FREUDIAN CRITICISM

Sigismund Freud, founder of the school of psycho-analysis was also a German speaking Jew. When he began to examine people who suffered from emotional disorders, he thought that he could identify a process which explained man's obsession with religion. Nature provides children with a mother and a father, but these parents sometimes go away and also often fall short of the ideal parent that the child would like to have. The child therefore *internalises* his mother and father and makes them larger and more perfect than any mere human figure. It is these internalised parent figures that emerge as gods and goddesses.

Unlike Marx, Freud did not want to see religion abolished. He felt that it was an essential prop to human life. But nonetheless, if accepted, his theory is bound to prove damaging. The great religious faiths which we have studied must surely stand or fall as being something more than a mere protection against the harsh realities of life.

THE SCIENTIFIC HUMANIST CRITICISM

In our first chapter we recognized that the fear of the unknown led primitive men into thinking in religious terms. In the last hundred years scientific advance in many fields has reduced the area of the unknown. We understand the causation of disease. We can see how life has developed by the evolutionary process. We no longer think of the planets and stars as mysterious heavenly lights. Some astronomers assert that it is unnecessary to think that the universe was created at any moment in time and biologists appear to be on the point of finding a scientific explanation for the origin of life.

We now recognize that the universe in which we live is immensely huge, and that man inhabits a tiny planet which revolves round a comparatively insignificant star on the outer edge of the galaxy known as the Milky Way. When

Yuri Gagarin went into space he reported to the people listening on the ground that he had reached the heavens and found no God. American astronauts have taken care to counter this, and one read the first chapter of Genesis from the moon's orbit.

Scientific humanists argue that man no longer needs to believe in a god. They would not, however, deny that the consequences of such a statement are somewhat daunting. The astronomer Fred Hoyle summed up his creed when he said that man is alone in a neutral universe. In this perspective the individual can no longer bask in his own importance or try to convince himself that his individual life has any eternal significance. It might be comfortable to believe in a God who cares for the sparrows as they fall, but, in the lack of any evidence of his existence, it is better to develop a sense of self reliance.

At the end of the 19th Century it was fashionable to say that science had proved religion to be wrong. Today most scientists would agree that this statement is not true. The religious questions which we have studied lie on a plane which science can neither prove nor disprove. It is perhaps more true to say that, for many, modern science has made religion appear irrelevant.

CONCLUSIONS

In our first chapter we recognized that religion did in some measure spring out of man's fears — his fears of the unknown, of pain, of death. In the advanced societies of today the sphere of the unknown is receding. Pain, at least in large measure, is defeated. Death remains with us, but we spin fairy tales and speak in euphemisms so that we can pretend that it does not exist. Perhaps one fear, above all, remains — the fear that our whole existence has no meaning. Watching crowds hurrying to work we wonder whether we are not all like hamsters on a wheel. Material standards of living and technological advance are now looked upon as ends in themselves, yet we have nagging doubts as to whether these goals are really worth all the striving that goes into achieving them. As the emphasis on success becomes ever more persistent, the temptation to 'drop out' becomes stronger.

The 20th Century has seen man split the atom and walk on the moon. It has not yet seen him answer that simple and fundamental question — 'Who am I?' This book has tried to look at some of the ways in which man has tried to answer that question. It does not claim to offer any final answer. 20th Century man may accept or he may reject the great religious systems of his ancestors, but he must surely accept the truth of the assertion that only the highest intensity of the sort of love that the great religious reformers have taught can penetrate the human condition.

Apollo 13 astronauts praying after a troublesome return to Earth

B. & T. Research